What they say about Dave Stewart

'If you are an entrepreneur and you spend time with Dave, you will know exactly what your next business idea should be. If you are a philosopher and you get talking to Dave, your mind will suddenly have clarity like never before. If you are a student and you listen to Dave, immediately you will believe in yourself and know exactly what you need to do next. Dave is a creative genius' **Simon Fuller, Founder and CEO of 19 Entertainment and creator of** *American Idol*

'Captain Dave is a dreamer and a fearless innovator, a visionary of high order, very delicately tractable on the surface but beneath that, he's a slamming, thumping, battering ram, very mystical but rational' **Bob Dylan**

'Dave is who we all want to be – living his dream and actually changing the world every day with his gentle inspirational genius' **Janice Vandenbrink, Senior Vice President of Global Systems at Visa International**

'Dave is a truly extraordinary blend of creative genius and businessperson with flair' **Rita Clifton, Chairman of Interbrand**

'Real creativity has me in awe, and Dave Stewart is one of the most thrilling creative minds I have ever met' **Anita Roddick, Founder of The Body Shop**

'When I met Dave he talked for 12 hours about the impact of digitalisation on the production and distribution of media. As a banker, I didn't know what the hell he was talking about – nor did anyone else. Over the next five years, we all found out' **Michael Philipp, Chairman and Executive Board Member of Credit Suisse Europe, Middle East and Africa**

'For over 30 years I have been working with creative people the world over; but none compare with Dave. His creative cup overflows with originality, profusion and, most importantly, generosity. He is undoubtedly a genius' **Andy Law, Worldwide Chairman, The Law Firm**

'Jack of All Trades, Master of All of Them' **Sunday Times**

'He's a One Man Advertising Think Tank' **The Daily Telegraph**

What they say about Mark Simmons and *Punk Marketing*

'Blunt, fair, fearless and outrageous – just like the marketing style they espouse' **Publishers Weekly**

'*Punk* reads like the insider wisdom your tattooed brother gave during your first nose-piercing session: "Don't show Mom, but the girls at school will dig it"' **Advertising Age**

'Taken together, their anecdotes show that truly original, engaging and – most important – surprising ads will always prevail, whether they're labelled punk or not.' **Business Week**

THE
BUSINESS
PLAYGROUND

FT Prentice Hall
FINANCIAL TIMES

In an increasingly competitive world, we believe it's quality of thinking that gives you the edge – an idea that opens new doors, a technique that solves a problem, or an insight that simply makes sense of it all. The more you know, the smarter and faster you can go.

That's why we work with the best minds in business and finance to bring cutting-edge thinking and best learning practice to a global market.

Under a range of leading imprints, including *Financial Times Prentice Hall*, we create world-class print publications and electronic products bringing our readers knowledge, skills and understanding, which can be applied whether studying or at work.

To find out more about Pearson Education publications, or to tell us about the books you'd like to find, you can visit us at **www.pearsoned.co.uk**

PEARSON

DAVE STEWART & MARK SIMMONS

THE BUSINESS PLAYGROUND

WHERE CREATIVITY AND COMMERCE COLLIDE

Harlow, England • London • New York • Boston • San Francisco • Toronto • Sydney • Singapore • Hong Kong
Tokyo • Seoul • Taipei • New Delhi • Cape Town • Madrid • Mexico City • Amsterdam • Munich • Paris • Milan

PEARSON EDUCATION LIMITED

Edinburgh Gate
Harlow CM20 2JE
Tel: +44 (0)1279 623623
Fax: +44 (0)1279 431059
Website: www.pearsoned.co.uk

First published in Great Britain in 2010

ISBN: 978-0-273-72688-3

British Library Cataloguing-in-Publication Data
A catalogue record for this book is available from the British Library

Library of Congress Cataloging-in-Publication Data
Stewart, David A. (David Allan), 1952-
  The business playground : where creativity and commerce collide / Dave Stewart & Mark Simmons.
    p. cm.
  Includes index.
  ISBN 978-0-273-72688-3 (pbk.)
  1. Creative ability in business. 2. Success in business. I. Simmons, Mark, 1963- II. Title.
  HD53.S738 2010
  658.4'094--dc22

                               2010010962

10 9 8 7 6 5 4 3 2
14 13 12 11 10

Text design by Design Deluxe Limited
Typeset in 10/14 pt Swiss 721 BT roman by Design Deluxe Limited
Printed and bound in Great Britain by Ashford Colour Press Ltd, Gosport

CONTENTS

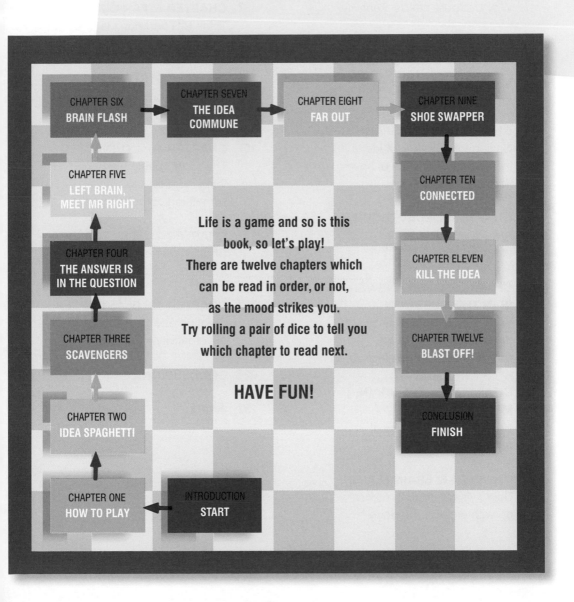

Life is a game and so is this
book, so let's play!
There are twelve chapters which
can be read in order, or not,
as the mood strikes you.
Try rolling a pair of dice to tell you
which chapter to read next.

HAVE FUN!

FOREWORD
Catching the cow

I am by nature an adventurer and am continually energised by whatever challenges I can find to throw myself into (sometimes almost literally), whether that's shaking up an industry or trying to circumnavigate the world in a hot air balloon. **It's the same enthusiasm and openness to new things that young children have.** When I was growing up, my family and I would often talk about business ideas at the dinner table and, because my parents made it so much fun for me and my sisters, that wonderful memory has stayed with me.

I set up my first business when I was 16, publishing a magazine. I really had no idea what I was doing when I started that venture, or my next one selling discounted records … hence the name 'Virgin'. I had what I thought was a good idea, but with little in the way of a business plan, and just went for it. Since then I've launched countless other businesses, some very successful (and a few that are best forgotten) and the Virgin name is now on everything from spas to spacecrafts.

I'm no longer a business virgin but the spirit with which I entered into my first few ventures remains. 'Catch the cow, Ricky', my mum used to say. 'If you want some milk you can't just sit in the middle of a field waiting for a cow to come to you, you've got to go and catch it and milk it yourself.' And that's what I've been doing ever since.

I'm lucky enough to have made a fair bit of money from my various ventures and could retire tomorrow, but because I'm doing what I love the thought of it never crosses my mind. I couldn't imagine not being part of that incredible buzz you get when talking about ideas and turning them into reality. That's what *The Business Playground* is all about – unleashing that creative power that's inside all of us and putting it to work to reach whatever business goals we have set for ourselves.

I've known Dave Stewart for 30 years, ever since he formed the Eurythmics with Annie Lennox, and have long admired him, not just for his musical talent, but also for his intuitive understanding of business. Like me, he gets really excited by big ideas and is always trying to find ways to make the best ones happen. At Virgin, if someone has a good idea, my first response is always 'Screw it. Let's do it.' and Dave is the exact same way.

Dave and Mark's enthusiasm for creativity and how it can be applied in business leaps off every page. *The Business Playground* will bring out the creative child inside of all of us and I can't imagine many readers being left uninspired to try it out for themselves. Their mix of insights about creativity, revealing examples, anecdotes, interviews with creative thinkers and games make for an entertaining and informative read. If you get half as much out of this book as I did, you're in for quite a treat.

I've been playing in the Business Playground ever since those times spent at the family dinner table discussing business ideas, and I hope to be playing for many years to come. Let Dave and Mark be your guides to your own exciting adventures into the Business Playground.

RICHARD BRANSON

Acknowledgements

Our heartfelt thanks to the people we interviewed for the book:

Paul Allen, Mick Jagger, Freddie DeMann, Christian Audigier, Matthew Warchus, Tim Brown, Evan Williams, Tero Ojanperä, Danny Socolof, Ethan Imboden, Jill Dumain, Philip Hess and Kyle MacDonald.

Thanks to Bob Dylan for granting us permission to reproduce the lyrics to his song *Forever Young* and to the Rolling Stones for letting us use their Tongue and Lips logo.

Thanks to Bird Design for designing the illustrated characters, to Sy-Jenq Cheng for designing the board games, to Kori Bundi for taking the author photographs, to Jamie Bryant for the photography retouching and to all the other people at Weapons of Mass Entertainment for their help.

Finally, thanks to Pearson Education for their belief in this project and for their hard work and diligence in putting the book together.

Publisher's acknowledgements

We are grateful to the following for permission to reproduce copyright material:

The Rolling Stones' Tongue and Lip logo on page 2. The Rolling Stones' Tongue and Lip is a trademark of Musidor B.V.; The SENZ umbrella image on page 42 reproduced courtesy of SENZ Umbrellas.

The Little Boy by Helen E. Buckley on pages 18–20, reproduced with permission; Excerpt from *Being There* on page 117, Copyright © 1970, 1999 by Jerzy Kosinski. Used by permission of Grove/Atlantic, Inc. and Transworld (Black Swan); Extract on page 214 from 'The Weird Rules of Creativity', *Harvard Business Review*, September 2001 (Sutton, Robert 2001), Harvard Business School Publishing Corporation; *Forever Young* lyrics by Bob Dylan on page 232, Copyright ©1973 Ram's Horn Music. All rights reserved. International copyright secured. Reprinted by permission.

In some instances we have been unable to trace the owners of copyright material, and we would appreciate any information that would enable us to do so.

INTRODUCTION

Why business needs creativity.

What's the secret weapon that will give a business an unfair advantage over its competitors? No, we're not talking industrial espionage or insider trading, we're referring to creativity. More specifically, the ability to come up with ideas and to successfully bring them to life in the marketplace.

Actually, that's not really a secret at all. **Time after time, in survey after survey, executives say that it is creativity that will drive their businesses in the future.** A recent IBM study[1] of CEOs and senior managers highlighted the importance of innovative thinking as the world of business continues to change. Eight out of ten CEOs predicted significant change ahead; change that comes from just about anywhere. One of those interviewed described the business environment as 'a white-water world'. We don't think this was referring to an amusement park ride.

'Innovation in business offers an alternative to the endless downward spiral of commoditisation that comes if you don't,' says Tim Brown, CEO of IDEO, a top design and innovation consultancy. 'Once you're over a certain bar in terms of quality or efficiency, there's very little competitive advantage to be had from doing more of that. Everybody else learns just as fast as you do. The only alternative to commoditisation is new choices and alternatives that haven't existed before.'

In a 2008 Boston Consulting Group survey of senior executives from around the world,[2] two-thirds of them put innovation as one of their top three strategic imperatives. That's good, right? But, and here's the rub, less than half of the big cheeses questioned were happy with the results that their investment in innovation brought. According

[1]'The Enterprise of the Future: Global CEO Study', conducted by IBM and The Economist Intelligence Unit, 2008.

[2]'Innovation 2008: Is the Tide Turning?', The Boston Consulting Group, 2008.

to the report, these cheese blues came from a combination of the time it takes to develop innovations, risk-averse corporate cultures, not knowing which ideas to select to put money behind, and from internal shenanigans. In the words of Benjamin Franklin, the man on the hundred-dollar bill, 'Vision without action is hallucination.' More on hallucination in a later chapter …

Creativity is vital for successful business, yet all too often it's not part of the culture. **Most businesses just aren't designed for creativity. Instead, they tend to be efficient machines with established processes, systems and rules that allow little flexibility for the more unstructured thought that is necessary for ideas to form and flourish.** 3M, a corporation once famed for its creativity, began to focus on efficiency at the expense of creativity and is now trying to find its way again. 'Invention is by its very nature a disorderly process,' says CEO George Buckley.[3] The Post-it note was one of 3M's biggest breakthroughs, created in the company's heyday, and its inventor, Art Fry, now questions whether his innovation would have ever seen the light of day in an environment that embraces efficiency over experimentation. His view is, 'Innovation is a numbers game. You have to go through 5,000 to 6,000 raw ideas to find one successful business.'

[3]'At 3M, A Struggle Between Efficiency And Creativity: How CEO George Buckley is managing the yin and yang of discipline and imagination', Brian Hindo, *Business Week*, 11 June 2007.

Tero Ojanperä, Executive Vice-President, Services and member of the Nokia Group Executive Board,[4] told Business Playground: 'Companies typically always drive for the linear innovation, where they continue to do what they are doing, but just a little bit better. And that helps you to a certain degree, but ultimately there is a point where it produces so little that somebody comes with the non-linear thinking and they bypass you and you are left behind. That's why companies typically fail. They continue with the old trajectory of things.'

So how do we break out of that linear way of thinking and make creative leaps? **Creativity is about exploring the unknown and so it feels very risky.** It's tempting to cordon it off into certain departments, assign it to off-site meetings or outsource it to agencies and consultants. That's a shame, because we all have the ability to be creative. As Tim Brown of design consultancy IDEO told Business Playground: 'The myth is that you have to wear black turtlenecks and designer spectacles in order for you to be creative. Sure, some people are born with talent they exploit, but everybody to some extent can use creativity techniques to be more productive and have better ideas than they would otherwise.'

By not making creativity a part of everyday business we're missing a trick. Jack Welch, former CEO of General Electric, urged corporations to 'Use the brains of every worker. Make sure that it is the person with the best idea who wins. Reward and celebrate new ideas to encourage others to want to contribute as well. Reward

[4]Nokia is the biggest mobile-phone company in the world and, if Tero has his way, will soon be one of the biggest media companies in the world. Nokia is becoming a massive distribution network for all sorts of content (such as music, games and film), services and applications. Its *Comes With Music* service, for instance, allows people who buy certain Nokia handsets to have unlimited access to millions of music downloads for a fee that is already built into the price of their new phone.

those who live the company's values, show "guts", and, in doing so, make the numbers.'[5] We were all born with great creative skills, it's just that sometimes these skills get sidelined or smothered through the rigidity imposed by schools and in businesses. There's plenty of evidence that the parts of our brains responsible for the logical thought processes inhibit the ones where creativity occurs, and that without the freedom to play it is not allowed to flourish. Stuart Brown, an author who has studied the 'play histories' of 6,000 adults, says that 'Play-deprived adults are often rigid, humorless, inflexible and closed to trying out new options. Playfulness enhances the capacity to innovate, adapt and master change in circumstances. It is not just an escape. It can help us integrate and reconcile difficult or contradictory circumstances. And, often, it can show us a way out of our problems.'[6] Play doesn't just give the brain a rest; 'Play is an active process that reshapes our rigid views of the world,' he says. **Playfulness is a vital ingredient of creativity and one that is often at odds with the serious environment of the business world.**

The Business Playground[7] aims to change all that. In the next twelve chapters we are going to look at what it means to be creative, from our own perspective (with additional personal anecdotes on the side from Dave) and those of some highly successful artists and entrepreneurs. Mixed in with these are research studies and a bunch of games and techniques we hope will give you a fun way of unleashing your amazing creative potential and applying it to business. Are you ready to play?

[5]*Jack Welch & The G.E. Way: Management Insights and Leadership Secrets of the Legendary CEO*, Robert Slater, McGraw-Hill, 1998.

[6]'Let the Children Play (Some More)', Stuart Brown, *The New York Times*, 2 September 2009.

[7]Sadly 'business' and 'playground' are two words you don't often find together in the same sentence – they somehow seem contradictory – but we think they need to become firm bosom buddies.

CHAPTER ONE
HOW TO PLAY

When we unleash our
natural creative potential,
anything is possible.

There was no grand plan to what the Rolling Stones did, they just wanted to make great songs and music and they threw their hearts and souls into it. They were *Tumbling Dice*.

This unbridled creative spirit has made them one of the most enduring and iconic brands. It wasn't all down to chance, of course. Mick Jagger, in a recent interview, told Business Playground, **'Very early on I think I realised that image-making was as important as the music. Visual imagery helps tells the story.'** He commissioned the Tongue and Lips™ logo for a Rolling Stones record label and it has since become one of the most recognised images in music history. Created by John Pasche, a design student who was still at the Royal College of Art when he got the call from Mick's office, it was inspired by Mick's mouth and was a perfect visual summation of the band's anti-authoritarian image. It was first used on the inner sleeve of the 1971 album *Sticky Fingers* (Andy Warhol did the cover art) and then as a design element on a slew of other record, CD and DVD covers and merchandise. The Rolling Stones were definitely the bad boys of rock at the time and Mick Jagger immediately saw the beauty of the simple yet iconic design. Mick was very knowledgeable about design. According to Pasche in a recent interview[1] about working with Mick: 'He's always taken a lot of interest in everything graphical and photographical related to the band and he understands the importance of image,' and when he was satisfied with a piece of design work, 'he would get the rest of the band to rubber stamp it'.

[1]*Creative Review*, 2 September 2008.

WHAT'S THE BIG IDEA?

John Pasche had a great idea for a logo and the Stones recognised its power. Every one of us has ideas every day: ones like, 'I know, I'll go and get a coffee now, one with froth and chocolate sprinkles'; or, 'I think I'll wear the tie with little fishes on it today. People made fun of me when I wore it last time, but they can go stuff themselves.' As ideas these are hardly earth-shattering innovations, they are just thoughts that pop into our heads. Then there are things we do which aren't ideas, but can loosely be described as creative. We doodle in meetings, we make jokes and we help with our children's craft projects. Again, nothing that will bring us fame and adulation, but we've at the very least made something from nothing that has some sort of meaning to us, and possibly to others.

Creativity is more than the production of ideas; the ideas have to be novel and useful as well. Unrealistic or unoriginal ideas are two a penny (the exchange rate fluctuates according to economic circumstances), while practical and original ones are a little harder to find. For instance, take Thomas Edison's incandescent electric light, an idea he patented in 1879. (Actually, the first incandescent light source was developed by Humphry Davy in 1809.) It became the first 'arch lamp', which then became abbreviated to 'arc lamp' when the marketers got a hold of the idea. Attempts to roll out arc lamps commercially weren't successful because of the lack of a constant supply of electricity. It wasn't until Edison developed a system to supply electricity all over the place that the incandescent light became practical on a large scale. The point is, Davy's invention wasn't that useful until Edison found a way to make it so. Edison promised: 'We will make electricity so cheap that only the rich will burn candles.' And he did. Competitors were incandescent with rage (excuse the bad pun), especially rival inventor William Sawyer who claimed Edison had infringed his patent.[2]

And then there's the novelty or originality of the creative output. **Music is a great example of creativity at work but, more often than not, even the most incredible musicians start their careers by playing music that isn't their own.** The Beatles were naturally gifted musicians and right from the beginning of their careers, first as The Quarrymen and then as The Silver Beatles, they demonstrated an amazing raw talent. To start with, though, the songs they played were covers of other people's songs, and while the lads certainly demonstrated their own distinctive style and flair, there was a long way to go before they would reach their full creative potential.

In their early days John and Paul would write songs that sounded like all of the other songs they had been playing at Liverpool's Cavern Club or in the Hamburg clubs, where they would often perform throughout the night. But after a lot more practice at songwriting they got better and better at it until, at last, they were able to produce truly original songs, many of which, of course, immediately became classics.

Their first hit was in November 1962,[3] and over the next eight years[4] they produced some of the finest popular music ever created. One album in particular stands out; on 1 June 1967 The Beatles released

[2] According to Wikipedia (**http://en.wikipedia.org/wiki/Thomas_edison**), 'On 8 October 1883, the US patent office ruled that Edison's patent was based on the work of William Sawyer and was therefore invalid. Litigation continued for nearly six years, until 6 October 1889, when a judge ruled that Edison's electric light improvement claim for "a filament of carbon of high resistance" was valid. To avoid a possible court battle with Joseph Swan, whose British patent had been awarded a year before Edison's, he and Swan formed a joint company called Ediswan to manufacture and market the invention in Britain.'

[3] *Please Please Me*, their second single, was released in November 1962 and went to Number 2 in the UK charts.

[4] Paul filed a suit for the dissolution of the band on 31 December 1970.

Sgt. Pepper's Lonely Hearts Club Band. This was such an original album, chock-full of ideas, experimental recording techniques and unique songwriting. They had begun to understand what a truly original idea was, and their fans could hear it in the music. The day the album was released it could be heard blasting out of houses, bedsits, apartments and palaces all over the world. They had practised so much at being creative that on *Sgt. Pepper* they broke through *the brain barrier* and delivered a pop music masterpiece.

The album inspired other musicians as well as fans. Jimmy Hendrix learned the whole album the day it was released, and just three days later at a gig at the Saville Theatre in London, much to the amazement and delight of an audience that included Paul McCartney and George Harrison, he performed his own version of it. Jimmy had no trouble in letting his creativity flow. He also knew that the more you practise being creative the better you get at it. As The Beatles proved, when we combine the process of creativity that we all innately have with our ability to come up with original ideas, you have the power to transform. **And in business, when the idea serves a useful purpose that meets specific needs, this can mean transforming products, market sectors and even whole industries.**

CREATIVITY IS CHILD'S PLAY

'Every child is an artist. The problem is how to remain an artist once we grow up.' Pablo Picasso

Saying creativity is child's play is not to say it's easy, but to children it's second nature. It's what they do: they explore, they question,

Whether an idea is novel and useful to you depends on the purpose of your creation. Sometimes it's just to fix your own shoe or some contraption so you can read in bed a bit better. My stepfather, Julien, had amazing ideas every day and he put them to good use. He never worked, was a practising Zen Buddhist (his own version) and he never touched money. Julien would only eat, read or play with what he found each day and he was a recycling genius. He also was a true pioneer against global warming. Back in 1970 he was marching up and down Hampstead High Street and Downing Street wearing his home-made sandwich board on which he had written: 'The ice caps are slowly melting. We are all in grave danger.'

I'd go visit him and he would be sitting on the floor wearing a paper Christmas hat playing electronic chess with himself and eating salami, all three things he had just found thrown away locally on his morning stroll. But I was more fascinated with some of the things he invented out of these discarded objects. He would struggle home with old chair legs and coat hangers, 500 door handles, all sorts of stuff, then the next time I went to see him (he lived with my mum around the corner in Maida Vale in London) he had turned these bits and pieces into fantastic inventions, some of which would have sold like hotcakes if they went into production, and he had already built the prototype.

Most of these prototypes were built out of necessity, as he was quite lazy and had bad vision so he wanted things to come to him as opposed to getting up to get them – my favourite was his Aphrodisiac Bedside Lamp. He had found a female dummy's leg that they use in shop windows to display nylon stockings and he had then found a light bulb, a cord and plug and a lampshade. A brand new pair of stockings and, hey presto!, in a few hours he had it all working. He said, 'Just imagine, now every night to turn out the light I have to reach my hand inside a lady's skirt, touching her stocking, and grope around for the switch.'

Now that is as good as any pill on the market today! You see, Julien was using creativity to solve every one of his problems and to satisfy all his wants. He lived like a king on creativity, and he didn't ever need to even cash a cheque!

they build and they destroy and the next minute they do it all again. As we get older, things get in the way of our creativity. We learn rules. We have to go to school. We get a job. We fit in and conform. And, little by little, we forget how to do it. Evan Williams, co-founder and CEO of Twitter, told Business Playground about his experience of school in rural Nebraska: 'At grade school my parents were told by my teachers I would come up with the right answers but the wrong way. Even if I knew the answer I didn't want to get to it the way they wanted me to get to it.' He says, **'I definitely think people can learn how to be creative, but I think for the most part people unlearn how to do it.'**

Creativity and education expert Sir Ken Robinson writes[5] and talks about the amazing creative abilities of children and the confidence they have in them before they are often knocked back by the adult world. In a speech at a recent TED conference,[6] an organisation founded around big ideas, he tells the story of how a little girl has so much conviction in her own imagination and ideas. She is busily drawing away in class and her teacher asks her what she's drawing, and she explains that it's a picture of God. The teacher tells her that nobody knows what God looks like. 'They will in a minute,' the little girl says. In fact, data shows how as children get older they lose their ability to think divergently (see Chapter 2), which is a key component of creativity: 98 per cent of three- to five-year-olds tested showed they could think in divergent ways, but by the time they were 13 to 15 years old, only 10 per cent could think in this way. And when the test was used with 25-year-olds, only 2 per cent could think divergently.[7]

[5] *Out of Our Minds: Learning to be Creative*, Ken Robinson, Capstone Publishing Limited, 2001.

[6] **www.ted.com/index.php/talks/ken_robinson_says_schools_kill_creativity.html**

[7] 'Creative Thinkers Wither With Age', Elizabeth Bule, *The Times Educational Supplement*, 25 March 2005.

Multi award-winning film and theatre director, Matthew Warchus (he won the 2009 Tony Award for Best Direction of a Play for *God of Carnage*), told Business Playground about his experience at school: **'I've often thought that the arts are a great recycling centre for people who've got certain aspects in their personality that might be seen as dysfunctional in other areas,'** he told us. 'But, if you bring them to creative arts they find a fantastic role. My slight dysfunction is that I've always been a bit of a loner and an outsider and I can remember most of my time at school being spent on the outside, looking in, listening to other people talk and behave together and not really being in the middle of anything.'

Fortunately Matthew found a career that was based on his ability to step back from things somewhat: 'Someone like me is used to being on the outside and having an overview of things, and is able to see patterns in behaviour and life and the interactions between people. In conversations you see patterns that you wouldn't notice if you were on the inside of the conversation. And that kind of person doesn't make a very good actor, for example, nor a very good orchestral instrumentalist, and that could be an unfortunate type of person to be if there wasn't a great job for that type of person, which is being a director.'

CAN CREATIVITY BE REDISCOVERED?

If we don't make use of our creative skills they become weaker. But are they still there when we're older?

The Moon and Sixpence[8] is a short novel by William Somerset Maugham, based on the life of painter Paul Gauguin. The story is about Charles Strickland, a stockbroker who, like Gauguin, leaves his family to purse a passion for painting. After a number of years

Until a certain age children are not hampered by self-doubt. My daughters Kaya (10) and Indya (8) are constantly solving stuff through creative 'brainsailing'. To them everything is easy peasy.

Recently Kaya was in the car coming home from school and she was saying that the teacher was telling them that there needs to be more awareness about recycling and everyone should try to 'go green'. As she was telling me this we were stopped at a traffic light on red. When the light turned green Kaya immediately connected the dots and said, 'Why don't they write recycle on every green traffic light!'

So simple, and a brilliant way to brainwash everyone on the planet, plus it would be cheap and easy to do. In fact, after I write this I'm going to approach Mayor Villaraigosa in Los Angeles to ask if we can do a test in a small area.

living in poverty in Paris, Strickland makes his way to Tahiti where he eventually dies from leprosy (oops, sorry, we just gave away the ending). His greatest work of art is the one he paints on the walls of the hut in Tahiti in which he lives. But because he has no visitors to his remote part of the island, thousands of miles from civilised society, nobody from the outside world ever gets to see it. Following his instructions after he dies, his Tahitian wife burns down the hut leaving no trace of his life's work. The creativity was there in Strickland throughout his dull life as a stockbroker and eventually it broke free.

[8]The title of Maugham's book is thought to come from an earlier novel he wrote, *Of Human Bondage*, in which the main character is described as 'so busy yearning for the moon that he never saw the sixpence at his feet'. For both the fictional character, Charles Strickland, and for Paul Gauguin, the real artist Maugham based the story on, the desire to create was more powerful than the comfort and security of family and a steady job. Both went for the moon instead of the sixpence.

There is compelling evidence to suggest that there remains a creative force in all of us. It's there, waiting to be used, but it is sometimes buried deep down or even repressed. It is a hidden, and for the most part untapped, reserve of creative energy that can sometimes be brought out under the most extraordinary circumstances. For instance, there are cases of people who had shown little or no creative talent until they started suffering from a mental condition called frontotemporal dementia (FTD). This condition forces parts of the brain involved in creativity to step in to compensate for deterioration in other parts of the brain. In FTD the temporal and frontal lobes of the brain are damaged and, when the left temporal lobe – the area responsible for speech, social behaviour and memory – is affected more than the right lobe, sufferers experience loss of memory and reduced verbal and social abilities. In fact, before being diagnosed with FTD it is not uncommon for sufferers to have been arrested for disorderly behaviour.

However, in addition to being thrown in the clink for a night, many of them go on to experience an increase in creative abilities. One sufferer, Jancy Chang, started to paint when she started suffering from FTD and, according to neurologist Bruce Miller, 'The more she lost her social and language abilities, the wilder and freer her art became.'[9] Another sufferer started to compose music despite having no musical training. And yet another patient, like Charles Strickland and Paul Gauguin, had been a stockbroker and when he became ill started painting, going on to win several prizes for his work. Miller believes that as people like these lose the ability to use words to conceptualise things they are forced into a much more visual way of thinking about the world. It's as if the brain, unable to operate through the usual means, compensates in other ways. Because parts of the brain's left hemisphere aren't functioning, parts of the right come into play, and these are the parts used in creativity. Miller describes the left hemisphere as a bully that suppresses some of the right hemisphere's musical and visual abilities, and when it's turned off the abilities then appear.

Other evidence[10] supports the idea that we retain the ability to be creative as we age; the quantity of creative output might decrease but the quality probably won't. **While adult creativity peaks in our 30s and 40s, there are late bloomers who peak much later – there is often a secondary peak in the late 60s.** So yes, even when we're older our creative abilities are still lurking down there, waiting to be reawakened. And the good news is that there are ways to tap into our innate creative abilities that don't involve leaving our families and jobs or suffering from dementia. We can exercise our creative muscles so they become strong again, as strong as they were in childhood when our imaginations were unbridled and the left hemispheres hadn't had a chance to bully them into submission.

THE PYRAMID OF THE POWERLESS

Of course, most businesses aren't designed for creativity. They tend to be designed to be efficient machines with established processes, systems and rules that allow little flexibility for the more unstructured thought that is necessary for ideas to form and flourish. **Even if individuals do find room for maverick thinking in corporations it is rarely encouraged or rewarded and employees often need to leave to become entrepreneurs.**[11] Many corporate environments make it almost impossible for good ideas to make it

[9]'Unleashing Creativity', Ulrich Kraft, *Scientific American Mind*, April 2005.

[10]'Creativity in Later Life', D.K. Simonton, the Theme Issue of *GENERATIONS 15*, no. 2, Spring 1991.

[11]Some companies, most famously Google, recognise this and encourage employees to devote a proportion of their time to pet innovative projects that the company will support and fund if they have merit.

out alive. The idea, often created by some underling far down the food chain, might never survive through the multiple layers that exist between him or her and the big boss. At each layer there are people who have the power to say 'no', but very little power to say 'yes', and so the idea dies before it ever gets to the decision-maker. As Charles Kettering, inventor of the starting motor and other useful stuff, said, **'If all the naysayers had to be met, nothing would ever be invented.'**

WELCOME TO THE PYRAMID OF THE POWERLESS.

CEO needs ideas

Naysayers

Underling with an idea

So the rubbish bins of corporations everywhere are full of the rejected ideas of dejected innovators. We don't think it has to be that way.

MOVE ONE SPACE FORWARD TO THE NEXT CHAPTER ... OR ROLL THE DICE

In this chapter we've talked about the importance of play for creativity. Freeing our minds from the shackles of linear thinking allows us to explore ideas and can result in the most amazing creative output. Music is a pure example of creativity at work and is a great way to illustrate the power of truly transformative and original ideas to break through and affect millions of people. All of us, regardless of whether we have artistic talent or not, have the power to be creative. We had it as children, but over time it can get buried by being undervalued or sidelined. Data shows there is a significant drop off in our ability to think divergently as we grow up, but there's also strong evidence that the creative abilities remain. Given the importance of creativity for business, it needs to encouraged so that it becomes an integral part of what businesses do. **Creativity can seem a little frightening and there are often sizeable barriers to new ideas making it through, but for businesses to thrive we need to embrace it and let it come out to play once more.** In the next chapter we explore what the ingredients are for great creative output or, as we like to call it, *idea spaghetti*.

"I think we all have been through this one. You want to get your idea or concept to a person that may comprehend it and above all has the power to implement it. This person is usually very busy, surrounded by barking dogs, or has already had someone whisper in his ear that you are nuts, or someone you know has mysteriously told him the same idea a week earlier as their own.

In 1996 I had my own TV channel on the web. It was called SLY-FI. It was a weekly show and pretty crazy, I must admit. I was so excited about this censorship-free environment that I went wild. The show was basically me as the host wearing unusual headphones with aerials and I tuned into strange happenings on our planet. It could be The Edge from U2 scuba-diving and looking for Pierre, or artist Damien Hirst showing a scorpion coming out of his penis. The 100 or so people who had fast-speed broadband and who saw it flipped out. They either said it was the greatest thing they had ever seen or they sent threatening emails.

I thought – this is the future! Every artist will have their own 'world' on the web. It would be a subscription, or ad-revenue based, or á la carte sales, or all of these things, and would disintermediate[12] all the sneaky money-siphon tricks and the holder-uppers in the food chain so artists could have a direct connectivity with their fan base.

A film editor friend of mine who had created a virtual shopping mall where you would be able to sell real estate (like an early version of 'Second Life'), came to see me and, with my artists' worlds in mind, I suggested we build an artist world with streets and shops and every piece of media. We met with Deutsche Bank and they gave us money to build 'Eurythmics World'. This was finished at the turn of the millennium. Since then I have had to play the 'Pyramid of the Powerless' game with huge corporations and, each time I get near to my idea becoming a reality, there is another obstacle in the shape of a vice-president or a middle manager.[13] Because what I want to do is fair

---

[12]To disintermediate is to miss out the middle-man. Or woman. Or child.

trade for artists and for them to have a direct connection to fans, as you can imagine this is not something that a lot of entertainment companies want to see happen. But, they need to change their role. Record labels are already morphing into management, marketing and merchandise companies.

They can still have creative input, it's just that things now need to be transparent. Now there's a scary thought to any entertainment company! (See Chapter 6 for a mind map we did a few years ago to help figure out how this new transparent model might work.)

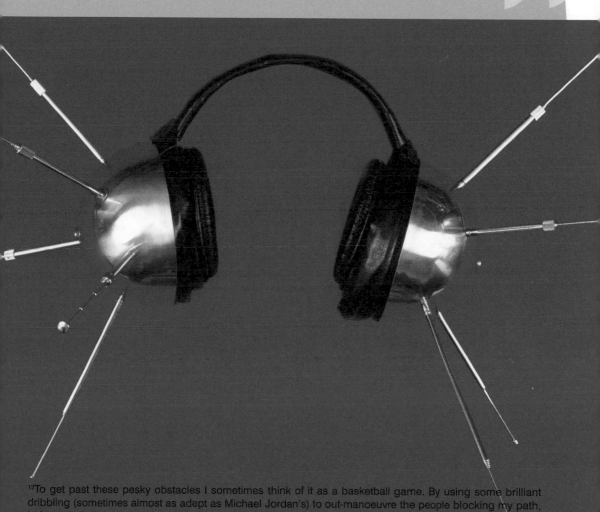

[13]To get past these pesky obstacles I sometimes think of it as a basketball game. By using some brilliant dribbling (sometimes almost as adept as Michael Jordan's) to out-manoeuvre the people blocking my path, I often still find a way to get past them and shoot a basket!

Instructions

1. Grab a die and some coins to use as counters.
2. Come up with a genius idea you want to sell to the CEO.
3. Take turns throwing the die and moving along the board.
4. Landing on certain spaces will shoot you up or send you down the board. Just follow the more detailed explanation on the following pages.
5. First to the top wins!

CEO

Boss went to an innovation seminar

Research it to death

Competition just did something clever

If it's such a good idea how come nobody's thought of it before?

Not created here

Death by committee

START

Dead PDA day

Offsite meetings all day MISS A TURN

Elevator pitch

How it works: Pushing an idea through an organisation is full of obstacles that must be overcome. Most of the time it's just like a game, and like any game worth playing, it helps to know the rules.

How to play: Players spend a few minutes writing down ideas for a new product on individual cards (see the game *Inspiral* in Chapter 10 for a way to generate some ideas), including a crazy name for it and a one-line description of what it does (e.g. 'Chewagloo', a blob of mint-flavoured glue that you activate by chewing). Players then each randomly pick an idea from the pile and try to make their way up the pyramid to the very top by throwing dice and, like in snakes and ladders, fighting obstacles and benefiting from helpful shoves along the way.

The helpful pushes:

'Elevator pitch': Land on this square and a player has 30 seconds to pitch the idea to the CEO's right-hand person (played by the person to the player's right, of course). To take the shortcut up the board the player must follow certain rules in his or her pitch: mention the name of his or her product exactly five times, use the words 'return on investment' twice and compliment the right-hand person on his or her appearance.

'Dead PDA day': There's been a glitch in the corporate software that has temporarily disabled everyone's smart phone, allowing them to get on with some work without being interrupted constantly and finding excuses to just check emails/voicemails/instant messages/you name it. This is a free ride up the board, so take it while the going is good – you just need to draw a quick picture of your product in less than 30 seconds.

'Boss went to an innovation seminar': Good for you, the boss has just heard about the importance of experimenting and taking risks with new ideas. All you need to do now to benefit from the boss's wonderful epiphany is to describe what the TV commercial for the new product will look like, and which celebrity will be the spokesperson for it.

'Competition just did something clever': The biggest competitor just launched a new product of their own and the CEO is on the hunt for ideas to show investors that your company can match those ne'er-do-wells move for move. You don't even need to do anything, just move up the board.

The obstacles:

'Death by committee': Land on this one and you have two minutes to answer the committee's (played by the other players) criticisms of the idea. Each committee member in turn must criticise the idea, starting with the words: 'It'll never work because …'. The player must respond to the criticisms using the phrase: 'I'm so glad you brought that up', and keep smiling throughout. The player will have to slide down the board if he or she doesn't answer, following this 'very strict' protocol.[14]

'Not created here': There's an unfortunate tendency to pooh-pooh ideas created by others. Land on this space and players drop down the board.

'Research it to death': Research has its place, mining insights about the people who might be customers for a product or service, but delegating decision making to market research is a surefire way to give it a slow painful death. Sorry, if a player lands here he or she will need to slide back down the board.

'If it's such a good idea how come nobody's thought of it before?': This often-heard justification for not pursuing an idea makes as much sense as wooden trousers. Maybe nobody has thought of it before because they're not as brilliant as you are, or because someone had said, 'If it's such a good idea how come nobody's thought of it before?' and they actually listened. The only way to escape certain relegation on this one is to throw a six with a die, otherwise you drop down.

How to win: Be the first to get to the CEO at the top of the pyramid. You're now the king of the castle and everyone else is a dirty rascal.

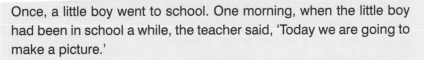

THE LITTLE BOY

By Helen E. Buckley

Once, a little boy went to school. One morning, when the little boy had been in school a while, the teacher said, 'Today we are going to make a picture.'

'Good!' thought the little boy. He liked to make pictures. He could make all kinds: lions and tigers, chickens and cows, trains and boats. And he took out his box of crayons. And he began to draw.

[14]It's up to you and the other players how strict to be.

But the teacher said, 'Wait! It is not time to begin!' And she waited until everyone looked ready.

'Now,' said the teacher, 'We're going to make flowers.'

'Good!' thought the little boy. He liked to make flowers, and he began to make beautiful ones with his pink and orange and blue crayons.

But the teacher said, 'Wait! And I will show you how.' And it was red, with a green stem.

'There,' said the teacher, 'Now you may begin.'

The little boy looked at the teacher's drawing. Then he looked at his own flower. He liked his flower better than the teacher's. But he did not say this. He just turned his paper over and made a flower like the teacher's. It was red, with a green stem.

On another day, when the little boy had opened the door from the outside all by himself, the teacher said, 'Today we are going to make something with clay.'

'Good!' thought the little boy. He liked clay. He could make all kinds of things with clay.

Snakes and snowmen, elephants and mice, cars and trucks. And he began to pull and pinch his ball of clay.

But the teacher said, 'Wait! It is not time to begin!' And she waited until everyone looked ready.

'Now,' said the teacher, 'We are going to make a dish.' He liked to make dishes. And he began to make some. They were all shapes and sizes.

But the teacher said, 'Wait! And I will show you how,' and she showed everyone how to make one deep dish.

'There,' said the teacher. 'Now you may begin.' The little boy looked at the teacher's dish, then he looked at his own. He liked his dish better than the teacher's, but he did not say this. He just rolled his clay into a big ball again. And made a dish like the teacher's. It was a deep dish.

And pretty soon the little boy learned to wait, and to watch, and to make things just like the teacher. And pretty soon he didn't make things on his own any more.

Then it happened that the little boy and his family moved to another house, in another city, and the little boy had to go to another school.

And the very first day he was there, the teacher said, 'Today we are going to make a picture.'

'Good!' thought the little boy. And he waited for the teacher to tell him what to do.

But the teacher didn't say anything. She just walked around the room. When she came to the little boy she said, 'Don't you want to make a picture?'

'Yes,' said the little boy. 'What are we going to make?'

'I don't know until you make it,' said the teacher.

'How shall I make it?' asked the little boy.

'Why, any way you like,' said the teacher.

'And any colour?' asked the little boy.

'Any colour,' said the teacher.

'If everyone made the same picture, and used the same colours, how would I know who made what and which was which?'

'I don't know,' said the little boy.

And he began to make a red flower with a green stem.

CHAPTER TWO
IDEA SPAGHETTI

Having lots and lots of ideas increases the chance of having some really great ones.

Remember Thomas Edison, the dude mentioned in the last chapter who invented the first viable electric lighting system? Turns out he also invented a bunch of other stuff too. Oh yes, Tom was no slacker. Known as 'the wizard of Menlo Park' (an area near San Francisco that happens to be just a couple of miles from Google Inc.[1]), he was one of the most prolific inventors in history, with a cool 1,093 US patents to his name, not to mention a few in the UK, France and Germany. In addition to electric lighting (1879), he invented the phonograph (1877) and the carbon microphone (also 1879, apparently a good year for Tom), which was used in all telephones for the next hundred years and in radio broadcasting.

Alex Osborn, known as the father of modern brainstorming, said that one key component of creativity is *fluency*, or how many ideas a person can generate. And Edison had this in spades. 'Prodigious' was his middle name (actually, Alva was, but let's not quibble). The other two components of creativity that Alex identified were *flexibility*, defined as the number of different types of ideas a person generates, and the *originality* of the ideas, or how unique they are.

Statistically speaking, which we try not to do too much, original ideas are those generated by less than 5 per cent of a sample. If, for instance, we were to ask 100 people for suggestions on what to do with a clothes hanger, the ideas that five or fewer of the people come up with will be classed as original (however bizarre the ideas are). Osborn claimed that fluency is the driver of both flexibility and originality. **The more ideas we generate, the more likely it is that the ideas will include ones that are varied and original.**

If coming up with so many ideas – what we call 'idea spaghetti' – is such an important driver, the question is: 'What helps make a lot of

---

[1] Don't you find it infuriating that the spellcheck on Microsoft Word's software still highlights 'Google' as a word it's never heard of? Competition, what competition …?

spaghetti?' The answer, it turns out, is not just having a big pasta pot to cook it in (though that helps), but instead the ability to think divergently. 'Meaning?', we hear you ask. Well, **there are two types of thinking: convergent and divergent. Convergent thinking is thinking that helps us converge on a single answer – e.g. 'the answer is 42'; while divergent thinking has many possible answers.**

Looking at things more broadly, as children do, is at the very heart of creative thinking, and asking open-ended questions is a good way to stimulate it. Say hotel guests are complaining they are having to wait too long for the lifts[2]; if thinking *convergently* the hotel manager might ask an engineer to fix the problem by installing costly new lifts. But by thinking *divergently*, the manager might reach a completely different and much cheaper solution to stop the guests complaining – for instance, by giving them something to do while they wait, such as magazines to read and mirrors to distract them. (We thought one of those 'what the butler saw' peep shows would also work, but that's just us.)

In the classic tale *The Little Prince*,[3] author Antoine de Saint-Exupéry tells the story of how, as a little boy, he drew a picture of a boa constrictor after it had swallowed an elephant. The drawing looked a bit like a brown misshapen hat, as a snake would look if it had swallowed anything that big. When he asked grown-ups whether the image frightened them, they answered, 'Frighten? Why should anyone be frightened by a hat?' Even his second attempt of showing the elephant inside the boa, this time from the inside of the snake, failed with the grown-ups. 'Grown-ups never understand anything by themselves, and it is tiresome for children to be always and

[2]Example from 'Creative Fitness', T. Verberne, *Training & Development*, 1 August 1997, pp. 68–71.

[3]From *The Little Prince*, Antoine de Saint-Exupéry (translation by Katherine Howard), Egmont, 1991.

forever explaining it to them,' says de Saint-Exupéry. Later in the book the Little Prince of the story's title, who is visiting Earth from asteroid B-612, talks about grown-ups and their ways: 'Grown-ups love figures. When you tell them you have made a new friend, they never ask you any questions about essential matters. They never ask you, "What does his voice sound like? What game does he love best? Does he collect butterflies?" Instead they demand: "How old is he? How many brothers does he have? How much does he weigh? How much money does his father make?" Only from these figures do they think they have learned anything about him.'

FOLLOWING TINKERBELL

Here's something interesting about these two different thinking styles – convergent and divergent – and how they can be used effectively. Evidence suggests that groups are better at convergent thinking, while individuals are better at divergent thinking.[4] When a problem has a single best possible answer, a group will work more effectively getting there than people working on their own do. But when many different ideas are required, a group comes up with more clichéd and traditional ideas compared to individuals. **Yes, contrary to the received wisdom, perpetrated we suspect by meeting facilitators and manufacturers of snack foods, group brainstorms are not always worthwhile.** In fact, bad brainstorms can be counterproductive, leaving participants feeling frustrated, confused and fat.

One reason for this is that groups generally try to avoid conflict, and yet by their very nature wildly diverse ideas are often in conflict with one another. The group tries to keep things on an even keel so that

[4]'Improving the Creativity of Organisational Work Groups', Leigh Thompson, *Academy of Management Executive*, 2003, Vol. 17, No. 1.

Most creative people like us have more ideas than they know what to do with. They will drive themselves crazy in the middle of the night trying to find a pencil and paper in the dark to make a note of the latest idea so they can fall back to sleep! Most of these ideas are great and you can spend hours discussing them over breakfast or in Starbucks after an espresso jolt. Only, after the espresso the idea you were talking about seems to morph into five other ideas, and in fact all of them are connected somehow to another idea you had three years ago.

By the time you've left Starbucks and fought through the traffic or climbed over 50 train commuters, balancing your briefcase and squashed sandwiches on your head, you've had a few more ideas about hover shoes and newspaper sandwiches that double up as news and breakfast and, before long, it's all turned into a Beatles' song and you are singing 'newspaper taxis appear on the shore' as you burst through the office door drenched from English summer rain. Of course, the office staff all think here comes that so called 'creative' nutcase again, singing with his sandwich on his head … why on earth do we pay him?

By the time our creative genius has got to his desk he has what we call *idea spaghetti*. In other words, a plate full of ideas but without a knife and fork! Now CEOs are often looking for ideas, but sometimes people hide the knives, forks and plates and the creative genius is left hyperventilating or behaving like an overactive puppy dog jumping up at anyone around him, yelping random bits of idea scraps or scratching and whining at the closed door of a CEO or chairman. We know there's a better way to keep the pot bubbling so that everyone gets some of that wonderful spaghetti.

the idea generation is a *pleasant* experience rather than a particularly *creative* one. People smile, they say nice things about one another's shoes, and come up with ideas that are all pretty much alike. In fact, participants often go through certain social rituals as if they were at a cocktail party. They tell stories, repeat ideas and make lots of positive noises: 'Hmm. That's a good one. Pass the chive 'n' onion oven-baked crisps, would you?'

Groups also have a tendency to slack off and only do as much, or as little, as the least productive person in the group. This is called 'downward norm setting', even if the slacker in question isn't actually called Norm, and alludes to the fact that the least productive members of the group have more of an influence on overall group performance than the high-flyers. And then there's the mix of distractions that come with working in a group. Just when you've started an interesting train of thought, some bozo interrupts with his or her own and by the time you've heard what they had to say your mind is blank again.

This is not a plea to work on your own when trying to solve creative problems. If some of these barriers can be removed, working in a pair or as a small group can be very effective. One way is to include a healthy mix of people from different backgrounds, or a mix of healthy people from different backgrounds. Ideally both. The point being, if they are *not* all people with similar ideas, interests, beliefs and love of bizarrely patterned socks, the chance for some novel ideas to bubble through is greatly increased. Another way is to give the participants in brainstorming sessions some high benchmarks to aspire to. Telling them how many ideas another group came up with, or telling them that their ideas will be posted for others to see, for instance, will bring out the competitive spirit in them and encourage them to come up with more ideas themselves – 'Sod those oven-baked crisps! I'll be dammed if those losers on the 12th floor come up with more ideas than us!'

Competition is good for the creative process, but the tendency for people to pooh-pooh one another's ideas simply because they weren't the ones who had thought of them – the 'not created here' syndrome – should definitely be avoided. The trick is to take the ego out of the process and to *follow Tinkerbell* (the fairy in *Peter Pan* [5]), the brightest light in the room. **If the group is rewarded as a whole for the best idea, then the participants will be motivated to build upon one another's ideas rather than do their best to ensure theirs is the one that wins out.**

Paul Allen, co-founder of Microsoft, clearly recognises the importance of group dynamics in creative thinking. In 2003, with a $100-million commitment, he founded The Allen Institute for Brain Science – a collaborative effort by a group of some of the world's top scientists to deepen our understanding of the human brain. In aiming at breakthroughs, as Paul told Business Playground, 'A lot of it's about bringing the right people together to become the optimal creative team.' The Institute's inaugural project is the Allen Brain Atlas, a geographic depiction of the mouse brain at the cellular level. By combining neuroscience and genomics to create a three-dimensional map of mammalian gene expression, the Atlas will provide invaluable insights into human disorders and diseases from Alzheimer's and Parkinson's to epilepsy, schizophrenia, autism and addiction. For the project to succeed, ultra-creative thinkers from different scientific disciplines need to work together. 'Everybody wants to say something, but you need people who will listen to each other, *really* listen, and understand where the other person is trying to go,' Paul says.

[5]Originally in J.M. Barrie's 1904 play and then his 1911 novel, *Peter and Wendy*, her name was Tinker Bell. For the 1953 Disney movie, *Peter Pan*, she was an attractive young blonde in a tight, lime-green mini dress and was modelled on the actress Margaret Kerry.

THE PERFECT BRAINSTORM

The *perfect brainstorm* removes the barriers to creativity by letting all ideas come out and be given a chance to breathe without the judgement and criticism that might otherwise kill them. It's like yoga without the grunting. **People, especially grown-up people, are afraid of doing something embarrassing in a group of peers (although that doesn't quite explain the popularity of reality TV or talent shows).** Tim Brown of IDEO talks about a creativity exercise that Robert McKim, founder of Stanford University's Product Design Program, would often use to prove this to a class of adult students. He would give them each a piece of paper and a pencil and ask them to draw, in just 30 seconds, the person sitting next to them. At the end of the time limit their sketches would, of course, be crap. And then they would invariably apologise to the person they drew. 'Yes, I know – sorry!'

Ask children to do it and they won't be embarrassed by their unflattering attempts to capture the looks of their peers. Have they no manners? Or, more likely, have they not learned to be afraid of the opinion of others? For grown-ups who expect rules, establishing some for creativity is important. One being: 'No idea is a bad idea.' And, in that vein: 'Don't be insulted if I make your nose look big on a sketch I'm asked to draw. I'm not a very good artist. The time I was given wasn't enough. And, well, it *is* kind of bulky.'

Both the setting of a brainstorming and how it is structured are important. To get the right brain to do its job, some form of 'meditative zoning out' is required so the left brain doesn't interfere before the ideas have been properly formed. Finding a space without too much formality or rigidity helps. Some wise folk have gone so far as to recreate the feeling of being inside a cloud by putting brainstorm participants inside a chamber made of billowing silk. Just imagine the ideas a formation of parachutists must have as they drift towards the ground under canopies of silk.

Once, about 15 years ago, I was up a tree house in Jamaica with a chap called Brian Reynolds. It was New Year's Eve, we were in Montego Bay and he wanted to be at his friends' party, at the Fault Line in Kingston, on the other side of the island. He also wanted to share New Year with his family in Yorkshire, and he also wanted have a jam session. Most people were saying he was crazy, and even I was doubtful, but he was so enthusiastic I followed him around, fascinated to see how he was going to pull this off and entertain us, his guests, at the same time. But lo and behold, by around 8p.m. that night I was talking to his mother in Yorkshire by video conference and even me and Brian sang a few Yorkshire songs with her while up in the tree house with a guitar and a computer. Then the Kingston party kicked in and Brian had a telephone dangling in front of the sound system in Kingston. He had dismantled it at our end and wired it through amplifiers and soon we were jamming with reggae band Third World playing live in Kingston and us playing live in Montego Bay, and laughing with his family watching in Yorkshire on a screen and drinking 'overproof' Jamaican rum!

Next morning, with a terrible hangover, Brian said, 'I think I will create a family of systems like this.' He was convinced this would be the future. And he registered the trademark iBook and patented lots of this stuff, such as interactive web books, voicechat and personas to text and converse with. Needless to say, given how what he envisioned has pretty much turned out to be reality, Brian is doing OK! And because he loves jamming so much he has now invented a way everyone can play real guitar easily using his own tuning method (take a look at **www.uplay2.org**).

IT TAKES TWO, BABY

Of course, there is a happy medium between working on your lonesome to come up with creative ideas and being part of a gang. And that's working with a partner. Many of the problems found with the group dynamic disappear while still providing the benefits of having someone to bounce ideas off and adding a different perspective. Think Rodgers and Hammerstein, Lennon and McCartney, Rice and Lloyd Webber, Bernstein and Sondheim, Black and Scholes, or The Captain and Tennille.

Paul Allen started Microsoft with Bill Gates, which made him one of the richest men in the world. As he told Business Playground: 'I was lucky to find an ideal partner in Bill Gates. He was more intrigued by the business side of things, and I wanted to focus on the technology side, so we complemented one another really well.' (For more of his interview, see Chapter 3.)

THE INNOVATION TRAIN

Tickets please!

Innovation never stops; it is an ever-spinning wheel. Think it's done? Think again. The cycle continues without faltering, like a toy train on a circular track, passing through the stations along the way. There's no last stop, just the station before the next one. When done right, the trip around the train track is fun. The stations will become as familiar as old friends, but the journey is always different. Who-oo whooooooo! Here's our track.

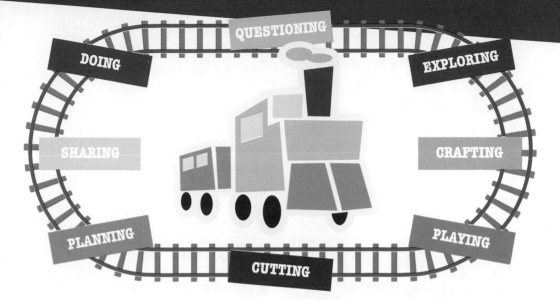

Each station along the way represents one of the eight key stages of innovation. Starting at the top:

Questioning What can be improved upon? What is it about a product or service or situation that isn't quite right? Why would anyone be interested?

Exploring What can we find out about it? What information is there about the thing we're trying to improve?

Crafting What's the best way to describe the problem we're trying to solve? How can we capture it in its simplest, clearest form?

Playing How can we solve the problem in a creative way? What creative techniques can we use to look at the problem in new ways and come up with innovative solutions to solve it?

Cutting What ideas should we focus on and which ones should we discard? Which are the ones that have the greatest potential for success?

Planning How do we put the idea into practice? What steps do we need to take, and who should we involve to help us?

Sharing What do other people think of the idea? How can we improve it so they are as committed to it as we are?

Doing Now we've answered all the questions, let's put the idea into practice.

And so it continues, on to the first station on the innovation journey again without stopping. Back to …

Questioning What can be improved upon? What is it about a product or service or situation that isn't quite right? Why would anyone be interested?

In this book we're going to take a stroll around some of these stations in a little more detail and introduce techniques to help make the journey go smoothly. Sandwiches and Thermos packed? Settled in a comfortable seat with a good view of the passing scenery? Let's go!

All aboard!

MOVE ONE SPACE FORWARD TO THE NEXT CHAPTER ... OR ROLL THE DICE

The more ideas we come up with, the more likely it is that one or two of them are going to be very good ones (now we know – size really does matter). So we need to do what we can to stimulate the creation of a ton of ideas, or what we call *idea spaghetti*, and that means thinking very divergently rather than trying to converge on one single answer. Brainstorms can be good ways to elicit divergent thinking, but they are a mixed blessing and can be counterproductive if not done right. The perfect brainstorm involves having clear parameters, including a mix of people from different backgrounds, encouraging a bit of healthy competition and setting high expectations for performance. **So creativity isn't about coming up with the one idea that will change the world, it's an exhilarating journey – the innovation train that never really ends.**

In the next chapter we go on a scavenger hunt for things to innovate.

I love bouncing ideas off inspiring people who also have spaghetti heads (or can cope with one). This could be anyone from a musician like Bono, The Edge and Bob Geldof, to film directors like Jim Sheridan or Shekhar Kapur, engineering or technology braniacs like Paul Allen or Nokia Exec Vice-President Tero Ojanperä. With people like these, it's a kind of ongoing conversation that never ends and it could be face-to-face in the middle of Africa or on a helicopter over a volcano in Hawaii … or in a fish and chip shop in Seattle. It could be via email or late-night phone calls, or in San Francisco sitting in Visa's boardroom with the CEO and CTO and the next day walking around Greenwich Village in the rain with Lou Reed discussing the same thing.

I've also been in floods and avalanches in Jamaica with the highly intelligent Shakira, and we never stopped the spaghetti-type discussions. In fact, Shakira and I carried on emails for a year afterwards in coded pasta conversations where she would sign off as Madame Tortellini and I would reply from the Linguini Brothers. My favourite to play 'wonky speak' with is Sam Roddick, with whom I have fast and furious iChats that usually leave us exhausted, ending in a brain orgasm. Sam is the creator of Coco de Mer (Erotic Emporiums) and I am fortunate enough to be a partner with Sam and her sister Justine in this sumptuous venture (never a bored meeting, I can tell you!). Sam and Justine are the daughters of Gordon and the late Anita Roddick, who founded the Body Shop, and Anita and I would often exhaust ourselves with brain-sparking sessions.

Instructions

1. Each player (from one to four people) picks a fork.
2. Agree on one topic that you want to come up with ideas for – choose from our list or make up your own.
3. Take a prong on your fork and follow the spaghetti until you locate the ingredient at the other end.
4. The number on the ingredient is the number of ideas you need to come up with in five minutes.
5. You get a point for every additional one you come up with, but lose one for every idea you are short of the target.
6. Play four rounds using different prongs and choosing different topics each time.
7. The winner is the person at the end with the most points.

BOARD GAME: IDEA SPAGHETTI

How it works: The more ideas we think up, the more likely it is we'll have a good one. In this game the object is not so much to come up with a solution to a problem but to train our brains (in fact, it's a 'brain-train') to generate lots of ideas (or spaghetti).

How to play: Players pick a fork and, by following the spaghetti strand to the ingredient it is attached to, see how many ideas they need to come up with in five minutes. In the warm-up round players should pick problems from the list below and then, when they've got the hang of generating lots of ideas fast, they can try it on a problem of their own choosing. They play four rounds, picking a different idea topic for each round and a different prong on their fork. They earn a point for every idea they come up with greater than the number they're required to, and lose a point for every one that falls below. So, if the ingredient says 12 ideas are required and they come up with 15 ideas, that's 3 points, but if they only come up with 10, they lose 2 points.

How to win: Players have five minutes per round, and after four rounds the player with the greatest number of points wins!

Another version of the game is a bit of a do-it-yourself game that doesn't involve a board at all, just some bits and bobs you should be able to find around the house. First, cut up some small pieces of card into the shape of ingredients – like mushrooms, tomatoes, ham, cheese – and write on each one a topic to generate ideas for. Challenges could, for instance, be coming up with 'new names for pasta', 'uses for a brick', or 'ways to generate power'. Players can choose to come up with their own challenges or use the list of suggestions given below.

Again, players will have five minutes to come up with as many suggestions (or as much spaghetti!) for each challenge as possible. But first the players have to pick up one of the ingredients from the bowl to decide which topic they'll be generating ideas for. Attach a metal paperclip to each piece of card and place all the ingredients on a plate or in a shallow bowl. Now find some small magnets (maybe from that Travel Scrabble set, or perhaps fridge magnets) – one per player – and tape them on to pieces of string. (How long is a piece of string? In this case, about the length of a strand of spaghetti.) Tie the other end of the pieces of string on to the prongs of some forks and – hey presto! – we're ready to play. Players simply dangle their spaghetti strands into the bowl to choose the ingredient they'll be using for their idea spaghetti.

Topics for ideas: Make me healthier; improve my neighbourhood; get-rich-quick schemes; impress the boss; work less; have more sex; use the car less; improve air travel; titles for a new movie; new names for pasta; ideas for new national holidays; ways to make me famous; save energy; fun excursions; titles for a new song; get more sleep; uses for a brick; names for a new restaurant; helping the homeless; theme hotels; reality TV shows that ought to be made; saving money; things they should teach in school but don't; generating power; April Fools' jokes; making parking easier; ruling the world; titles for your autobiography; saving water; odd adventure holidays; weird ice-cream flavours; silly gadgets.

CHAPTER THREE
SCAVENGERS

**Always on the hunt for
things to innovate.**

Nothing is perfect: no product, no service, no business model, no situation. There are always things that can be improved upon. The need to question and to wonder 'what can be changed?' is the engine for the whole innovation cycle.

Take outdoor clothing company Patagonia, for instance. Patagonia Inc. is a privately held company based in Ventura, California, and was founded by climbing enthusiast Yvon Chouinard. The stuff ain't cheap, but it is incredibly practical and well designed and so worth the cost. Patagonia also has a very strong social conscience with a mission statement that is clear and simple: 'Build the best product, cause no unnecessary harm, use business to inspire and implement solutions to the environmental crisis.' Patagonia strives to make each product with as little environmental impact as possible. They know that however hard they try, everything they do leaves an indelible footprint on the environment, and they are very open about the fact that they are by no means perfect. So they have found a way for consumers to track the carbon footprint of selected Patagonia products from inception to sale. For each one of the items they chronicle on the *Footprint Chronicles* microsite at Patagonia.com,[1] visitors can see the steps that Patagonia went through to develop it, and included with the facts and figures are short videos and pictures about the clothing's design, manufacture and distribution.

And this is not just a greenwash – there's bad news given alongside the good. For the *Nine Trails Shorts*, for example, the good news is that the factory has committed to stringent environmental and safety standards. The bad news is that the fabric the shorts are made from is neither recycled nor recyclable and, because the factory is in Vietnam, the finished product needs to travel no, er, *short* distance (sorry) to get to Patagonia's US Nevada distribution centre. In fact, each pair of shorts must travel 16,262km from the place where the

[1]On the US website it's at **www.patagonia.com/web/us/footprint/index.jsp**

raw material is sourced to the distribution centre in Reno, Nevada – that's a greater distance than that travelled when circumnavigating Antarctica (15,000km). Patagonia know they have more work to do to lower their environmental impact and they actively solicit feedback from consumers to help get there. Here's a big pat on the back, Pat.

Jill Dumain, Director of Environmental Analysis at Patagonia Inc., told Business Playground that what's been surprising about the initiative is not so much how well it's been received externally, but how difficult it's been for Patagonia employees to, as she puts it, 'learn out loud in public.' When the Footprint Chronicles initiative was first launched, employees felt they were on the front line in full public gaze, but management, convinced it was the way to go, pushed it through regardless. They wanted to take Patagonia's environmental commitment seriously, and they knew that if they just talked about the good things they were

doing they would only be telling half the story. 'We wanted to change the notion that we had it all figured out,' says Jill. The senior executives decided that to be part of a serious conversation about the environment they had to break through what she describes as 'the Patagonia Perfection Paralysis'. The culture had always been about doing the very best possible and employees found washing their clothes in public (see the section on metaphors later in the book) initially very awkward. But eventually, she says, the lack of self-censorship felt very liberating for them.

And it's forced everyone in the supply chain to think through what they do and the impact it has on the environment. **By looking at their carbon footprint in such detail they realised, for instance, that manufacturing locally is not necessarily the answer.** When Patagonia's top brass first conceived of the *Footprint Chronicles*, the received wisdom in the media was that it's got to be made locally to be green, so they were surprised to learn through their analysis how small, relatively speaking, the impact from transportation is – something they might otherwise not have known. 'If we'd simply listened to the environmental chatter,' says Dumain, 'we might have gone in a different direction.'

RIP IT UP AND START AGAIN[2]

One technique for looking at an existing product or service, and wondering how it can be improved, is to break it down into its components and then build it up again.

Figuratively, that is. This is sometimes called 'attribute listing', but we're going to call it Derek. Take a pen, for instance: a pen has a number of attributes, such as its look, its feel, what material it's made of, the type of ink it uses, how the ink is released so it stays in the pen when it's not needed and how it comes out when it is.

Or take restaurants: what are the different factors that make up the restaurant experience? The type of food, the price, style, and how it's delivered are some of the main ones, and each of these categories in turn has a number of different possibilities. The type of food, for instance – could be Italian, Chinese, Indian, English, Mexican, Middle Eastern, Thai, Japanese or Latvian, to name just a few. (You've tried Latvian, right?) Then, often independent of food type, there are the prices charged, which might be cheap, low priced, medium priced, expensive, or bleedin' pricey. Then there's the style of the restaurant: casual, formal, family-oriented or trendy. And how the food delivered could conceivably be by waiters on skateboards, eating it Roman-style while sprawled recumbent on soft pillows, as a take-away or home delivery, or even thrown by catapults (that could be fun!), We can make a list of each of these factors under their headings and then try different combinations of them to see whether one of them makes for a great new dining experience, or is in fact just a 'recipe for disaster'.

(Dave has a penchant for pricey Italian food served in a formal setting that he can take his time over; Mark for extra spicy Indian food washed down with icy cold beer.)

[2]I said, rip it up and start again.

FOOD TYPE	PRICE RANGE	STYLE	DELIVERY
French	Cheap	Formal	Skateboarding waiters
Italian	Low	Casual	Roman-style
Chinese	Mid	Family	Take-away
Indian	Expensive	Business	Home delivery
English	Boy, that's pricey!	Trendy	Catapulted
Latvian			

Try randomly picking from the different factors to see what you come up with. How about expensive Italian food delivered to businesses? Or how about mid-priced French food in a leisurely family-friendly restaurant? Nice one, Derek. And this same thinking can be applied to many types of business, especially those that sell products or deliver *experiences* in one form or another. The product can be broken down into the factors that fall within a small number of distinct categories, and these can then be recombined to create something completely new. (A giant triangular suitcase made of cotton wool was what we came up with, but don't tell anyone, it's still in development and it's going to be a big hit, we just know it.)

Another approach to innovation to see what needs to be changed about a product, a service or situation, is to think about the things that bug you about it. Take the umbrella (no, not *that* one, that's mine, the one by the lamp). The steel-ribbed umbrella was invented by Sam Fox[3] in 1852, although umbrellas in one form or another have been around for thousands of years. An innovative design, for sure, but not one without its flaws. It keeps the rain off and can be folded away to be put in a bag, used to fend off people when fighting to get on the bus or, when sharpened, even used to poison people with. But Sam's design is also prone to blow inside out or to break, and maybe even unintentionally poke out an eye or two.

[3]Sam Fox is also the name of a large-chested model who became famous by appearing topless in *The Sun* in the 1980s and 1990s, and more recently as a contestant on *I'm a Celebrity … Get Me Out of Here*, but it's not *that* Sam Fox. This one is Samuel Fox and, as far as we know, he never appeared topless in *The Sun* or on any reality TV show.

Dutch company SENZ Umbrellas designed a new umbrella that uses an asymmetrical (or 'lopsided') shape rather than a round one, apparently making it much more aerodynamic. It works with the wind rather than against it, and changes its orientation to deflect it without creating pressure on the fabric and ribcage. And those clever Dutchmen even added 'eye-savers' to protect innocent bystanders from being blinded. It was a roaring success. It went on sale in 2007 for $67 a pop and they sold 10,000 units in the first nine days.[4] Ophthalmologists were in uproar. SENZ[5] say their umbrella design 'makes Senz', which is a terrible pun, but we forgive them.

THE BUG LIST

The SENZ umbrella is so distinctive looking that, according to the company founders, its owners will stop and greet one another on the street (perhaps saying, 'I see you have plenty of SENZ! Ha!' but then again, probably not). Yes, SENZ designer Gerwin Hoogendoorn had come up with an innovative new design for an old product that had some inherent design flaws after he thought about the irritating and debilitating design flaws, or the bugs, of the original.

We asked SENZ co-founder, Philip Hess, why they picked the umbrella to redesign and not another product. 'Our journey started

---

[4]'The Umbrella Gets an Extreme Makeover: Dutch Designers Give Old Standby an Aerodynamic Twist', *ABC News*, 6 March 2007.

[5]You can see their umbrellas (for some reason not sponsored by Barbadian singer Rihanna, who had a hit with *Umbrella* in 2007) at **www.senzumbrellas.com**

out of pure frustration with traditional umbrellas,' he says. 'Everyone hates the fact that umbrellas always go inside out, break, poke you in the eye, provide bad visibility and are very uncomfortable.' As for the design process that led to the lopsided design: 'The process was never a Eureka! moment. First there was a solid analysis of all the problems people encounter with umbrellas. When coming up with solutions for all of those problems, although it sounds kind of corny, we really tried to go outside of the box, and we even considered magnetic fields and helicopter constructions above the head. However, as a designer you should also consider social acceptance and commercial potential. Therefore, the umbrella is still comparable to a traditional umbrella, but is fundamentally different. [Co-founder] Gerwin made the first prototypes of the SENZ umbrella by ripping apart old-style umbrellas and making asymmetrical umbrellas from them, using his grandmother's sewing machine!'

What's on your bug list? Bugs can be things you don't like about a product, a service, a whole industry, or just things that irritate the hell out of you.[6] Bugs that if you get rid of could be the basis for a wonderful innovation. For industrial designer Ethan Imboden a light bulb went off (a beautifully designed one, of course) when he realised that sex products needn't be ugly and cheap, and so he launched Jimmyjane as a range of very stylish alternatives made of precious metals. Some of the products even come with a small hole drilled into one end so they can be worn around the neck as a pendant, and celebrities like Kate Moss have done just that. Here's our bug list – feel free to steal any of them and send us your solutions (or better still, a royalty fee from the devices you invent).

[6]In the film *The Jerk* Steve Martin plays the character of a hapless chap, Navin R. Johnson, who invents an ingenious and stupid-looking device called the 'Opti-Grab', as a solution to the design 'bug' of spectacles sliding off the wearer's nose when the frames have lost their shape. Navin becomes rich beyond his wildest dreams. (For a while. He eventually gets sued and loses everything because a side-effect of the Opti-Grab was that it made people cross-eyed.)

- Junk mail.
- Piped muzak.
- Not enough time in the day.
- Air travel.
- Condoms.
- Parking.
- 'Special offers.'
- Commercial radio.
- Airport security.
- Shrink-wrapped packaging.

- Bottled water.
- Dog poop on the pavement.
- Tasteless fruit.
- Useless plastic toys.
- Customer service.
- Naysayers.
- Talking heads (not the band).
- We could go on ...

Oh, and did we mention the seats in coach class on aircraft? While we accept that the priority for the people who design the damned things is safety rather than comfort, comfort doesn't even seem to get a look (or knee) in. 'There is no catch-22 to this,' says Rick DeWeese, who is in charge of one of the Federal Aviation Authority's two crash-test centres. **'There's no reason a safe seat can't be a comfortable one.'**[7]

The people who make the seats for the airlines blame the airlines for packing the seats in too tight so passengers, squashed with a knee up each nostril and their elbows wedged beneath their armpits, can't wiggle about. The seats on their own are, according to the designers, just fine, it's just that if you have to stay sitting in them for too long without the ability to wiggle they become, well, a bit of a pain in the arse. 'If you put an economy-class seat in a nice place and compared it to an Aeron chair, I would argue that the Aeron chair is no more comfortable,' says Glenn Johnson, design director at B/E

[7]'Why Are Airplane Seats So Miserable, and What Can Be Done About It?', Eric Hagerman, *Popular Science*, 27 April 2009.

THE BUSINESS PLAYGROUND

Aerospace, which makes seats for Southwest Airlines, Continental Airlines and British Airways. Yeah, well, hmm.

The airlines, of course, blame the consumers, saying that more room for passengers to wiggle means fewer seats on the aeroplanes and less money for their coffers. But, luckily for us consumers, there do seem to be alternatives to the current seat design, ones that balance safety with comfort and the space they occupy, it's just that the ailing airlines will need to pony up and stick 'em in, so to speak. The *Cozy Suite*,[8] for instance, is a craftily configured seat row 'boasting', according to the company's website, 'a shoulder width as wide as business class'. It has a sort of staggered arrangement of seats so that each one is in a row positioned slightly behind the next. Other interesting designs that take a new approach to the traditional seating configuration include ones that use the vertical space above passengers to give them more room, and others that have passengers facing one another like on a military aircraft.[9]

Not accepting the way things are now is a great starting point for innovation. Even the humble mousetrap, the stuff of the innovation cliché, is the inspiration for countless new designs and patent applications. The saying goes: 'Build a better mousetrap, and the world will beat a path to your door.' The world excluding the mice, that is. As proof of this witness Rentokil who, in June 2006 and amid much fanfare, launched a digital mousetrap that tells operatives that a rodent has been caught and in which particular trap. The trapped mice or rats then go through some sort of interrogation, we imagine. They call their device RADAR – presumably the acronym preceded the choice of name – which stands for Rodent Activated Detection And Riddance.

[8]Developed by Thompson Solutions, a company in Northern Ireland that specialises in designing seats for the aircraft industry. Check out the Cozy Suite at **www.thompsonaero.com/cozy-suite.html**

[9]Designs by Emil Jacobs and by Design Q featured on *wired.com* in a feature by Jason Parr entitled 'Step Up, Lie Down, Sit Sideways As Airlines Explore Creative Seating', 8 October 2009.

Rentokil installed a bunch of them in Wembley Stadium and a press release from the following year boasting of RADAR's success proclaimed: 'As soon as a rodent enters the RADAR unit the pressure-sensitive pads detect its presence and automatically close the doors. The unit then releases a measured dose of carbon dioxide into the sealed chamber, killing the rodent quickly and humanely with no release of toxins.' And the blurb went on to say: 'With a capacity of 90,000, each event at Wembley Stadium will be a major catering exercise, and Rentokil will help keep the organisation free of harmful pests and the taint of poor hygiene that can go with them.'[10] You'd think they were talking about the fans.

BALL-GAZING

Looking into the future can help to focus the mind on what might need to be changed to help deal with it. Let's do some ball gazing to look at what life will be like in years to come. Gaze deep into the ball. Deep ... deep ...

OK, stop for a second.

A word of advice before we go on. **What life is like now shapes our view on what it will be like in the future, and so not looking far enough ahead tends to anchor our thinking to the present a bit too much.** Look just five years or so into the future and we tend to assume that it'll be like it is now, just more so. So if we don't look far enough ahead, it's likely we'll underestimate some big important shifts that will blow any current trends out of the water. These are the disruptions that force people to do things in a new way. Who, just a few years ago, would have predicted the explosion

[10]From 'Building a Better Mousetrap', Mark Roth, *Pittsburgh Post-Gazette*, 9 May 2007.

in social media, the collapse in the global economy or the rise of the tree frog as a superpower? These and other changes have fundamentally shifted the way we live our lives.

To clear the decks let's gaze a little bit farther forward, at least ten years into the future. Again, look deep … deep … That far ahead and it's easier to disregard the short-term trends and focus on a future that might be very different from the present. To help, let's throw in some big disruptive changes that might have happened along the way. For instance, the mists in the ball clear, and … it is the year 2025. Now,

- **People have lost the use of their legs.**
- **A scientific breakthrough has increased average life expectancy to 300 years.**
- **People rarely leave their homes because of dangerous freak weather conditions.**
- **Children are in charge.**
- **Women have declared all-out war on men.**
- **We have discovered the ability to read each other's thoughts.**
- **A team of mice are playing Chelsea in the FA Cup at Wembley.**

OK, so they're completely implausible (apart from the first, third, fourth and fifth scenarios, that is) but they will at least shake our minds free from the baggage of current experiences and how they limit our thinking. Maybe you could make the disruptive changes more relevant to your own situation? If it's business, what huge shifts can you imagine that could possibly happen in your industry? Not the little ones that are logical extensions of what's already going on, but the big breaks in the status quo. **Thinking through odd scenarios can help us come up with better ways to do or make something.** How odd you make them is up to you – throw a few in there that are on the crazy side. Here's one that could have been written 15 years ago that might have seemed crazy at the time, but it started to happen just a few years later.

You are a record label and in ten years' time people will have stopped buying your music because they can get it elsewhere for free.[11]

The music industry has had to adapt to survive and create new business models for itself as the sales of recorded music has dried up.

According to Irving Azoff,[12] a music industry goliath who, as CEO of Ticketmaster Entertainment[13] is reshaping the way the business works today, the revenue streams used to be record sales first, then ticket sales to live concerts, and third was merchandise. Sponsorship didn't even get a look in. But because over the past few years revenue from recorded music have plummeted, today sponsorship ranks only second to ticket sales as a revenue generator. The model has completely changed.

Through his company MEGA[14] Danny Socolof creates innovative strategic partnerships between artists – like Gwen Stefani, Led Zeppelin and Beyoncé – and brands including Pepsi and Cadillac.

[11]Shawn Fanning unleashed the music file-sharing site Napster in 1999.

[12]Irving Azoff was interviewed for 'The Price of the Ticket', John Seabrook, *The New Yorker*, 10 and 17 August 2009.

[13]In 2009 Ticketmaster, a ticket sales company, did a deal with concert promoter Live Nation and the new company is called Live Nation Entertainment. Seeing the writing on the wall, Madonna left her record label and signed with Live Nation Artists in 2007.

[14] www.megalv.com

He told Business Playground: **'The era of the album is dead.** There is a gigantic evolution going on in music today driven by many factors, the most important one being how technology is disrupting consumption patterns.' He cites Pandora Internet Radio as a great example of how things have changed.[15] Pandora lets people create their own radio stations (up to 100 stations per listener) of music they like by allowing listeners to plop in the names of artists or songs and then Pandora's software (called Music Genone Project) will play music with interesting similarities to the choice. Users can refine the stations so they more perfectly match what they want to listen to, and if they want to buy a song they can order a CD or purchase a digital download.

The Rolling Stones were way ahead of the game when they agreed to have their 1981 'Tattoo' tour sponsored. Mick Jagger told Business Playground: 'We did sponsorship for the first time and got a lot of attacks for it. It was a perfume company[16] and it was a real breakthrough,' he says. 'I don't think any tour had ever been sponsored before. They approached us and we said, "Well, why not? You know, we're not making a lot of money on this tour." In those days ticket prices were really low, so this would up the income. It wasn't very much money but it was a breakthrough thing. After that it became the norm, and the next time we went on tour we got more money from a much bigger company.' Most major tours and music festivals now have corporate sponsors attached.

Now, three decades later, artists are increasingly looking beyond sponsorships to more strategic partnerships with brands to help finance and promote their music. In 2008 the English electronic dance duo Groove Armada signed a revolutionary one-year deal with Bacardi in which the drinks company funded the band's new

[15] www.pandora.com

[16] The sponsor was perfume make *Jovan*.

recordings. Groove Armada gave Bacardi the rights to use the music, but retained ownership, created a web radio series and curated dance events for the rum brand. At the time Dan O'Neil, Groove Armada manager, said,[17] 'The old record company deal is a defunct model. Artists go away and sit in a studio for 18 months, they create an album – which people don't buy any more [because] they download individual tracks – and a large emphasis is still on how you get little plastic discs racked on a shelf. It just seemed wrong.' Andy Cato of the band explained that doing the deal was a big decision for them: 'There was a degree of nervousness about taking a leap so far away from anything that's gone before, but at the end of the day, we've got an amazing live show, one of the best in the world,' he said. 'We need to break that in markets where we need financial help … and as always we want to get our music to as many people as possible.'

Socolof thinks that music gives brands a perfect way to develop deep human connections with their consumers. He told Business Playground: 'All the technology in the world, as it relates to music, is meaningless unless human connections are made. Ultimately, music is the thing that resonates with people more than anything I know.' As an entrepreneur, Socolof knows that the first rule of success is that nothing stays the same: 'Change is never a good friend to people or institutions that are risk adverse.' But he knows how much more difficult it is for corporations to shift direction. His greatest successes have come from working with what he calls internal entrepreneurs (we call them *intrepreneurs*). 'Internal entrepreneurs know that real innovation and breakthroughs don't come without risk – whether they've been given permission to take the risks, or have just taken it.'

[17]'Duo's Revolutionary Pact with Bacardi', Paul Sexton, *Financial Times*, 17 April 2008.

Groove Armada, like the Stones, have found smart ways to finance their music that embraces change rather than fights it. When Business Playground interviewed Tero Ojanperä, the Executive Vice-President, Services at Nokia, he talked about the need for disruptive factors such as technology to be embraced as positive agents of change and not to be feared: **'Technology is moving so fast nowadays and when it comes to mixing technology and art and creativity, people tend to fight the technology. They think there is something bad and it's like "destroying my business, it's harming us", but very often if you embrace it sooner rather than later you will find out that it unleashes completely new forces in creativity.'**

We are currently working on a smart way to match up artists with corporate sponsors. 'Sponsorbility' will use a sophisticated online database to allow brands to search for musicians and other artists that they are willing to help support in exchange for sponsorship rights. Say, for instance, there's an up-and-coming band that has a bit of a following but needs a few thousand quid to record an album to sell on iTunes, and a local chain of fish 'n' chip shops decides to stump up the cash, the band could play gigs at the shops, allow the chippies to use the music in radio ads and offer discounted merchandise at live events, and music and merchandise to the shops' regulars. A system like this, if easy to use, will be a clearing-house to match opportunities that work for both the artists and the sponsors.

YOUR BIG GREY SPONGE

As Albert Einstein said, way before the invention of the Internet, 'I have no special gift, I am only passionately curious.'

The brain is a big, blobby sponge ready to absorb all that comes its way, and creative types are more often than not avid consumers of information and entertainment.[18] They read all sorts of media, go to movies, listen to music and podcasts, scour websites. They always hunger for *more*; they never feel that they know enough.

Paul Allen, co-founder of Microsoft, told Business Playground how these habits ran deep with him: 'I guess it started when I was a kid. Both my parents were librarians, so I was always around books. When I got a little bit older, I devoured magazines about computers and technology, just stuffed my brain with everything I could learn about technology and the future. I still read everything I can get my hands on … and every now and then you see a connection of two ideas, where the link transcends the individual elements. With Microsoft, the critical connection was between a microprocessor and an easy-to-use programming language called "BASIC".

'That turned out to be a pretty good idea![19]

'Those big ideas don't come to you every day – it has probably happened to me ten times in my life, at most. When one pops out, first you have to check to see whether anyone else is already on the same trail of thought. If the way is clear, you need to jump on the opportunity.

---

[18]To have a look at some of the websites we peruse on a regular basis to feed our minds, go to **www.businessplayground.com**

[19]It was the idea that spawned Microsoft.

'What does it take to make a breakthrough? A certain natural curiosity – and, just as important, a fearlessness to put your idea to the test. Luckily, I've had both of those things. It might be genetic or the way you're brought up, but you have to have an incredible *thirst* to take in what's out there, which paves the way for the next step. In your case, I'm sure you [Dave Stewart] studied 30 different guitarists and all their licks, and learned all The Beatles' songs down to the last note – and that made your imagination more fully formed. I read shelves of science fiction when I was young, which was great training for my brain. It led me to think of things that didn't exist, or "might" exist, or *shouldn't* exist, even.

'Some people are focused and deep in one or two areas. I'm different in that I'm interested in so many different things, from brain science and rocketry to professional sports franchises and underwater exploration and software. **For me, life is a rich and complex gumbo; there are so many things to explore in the world.** Entrepreneurial ventures are especially fascinating to me, even when they might seem mundane from the outside. When I was involved with Ticketmaster, which on the surface seems like a simple business, I got excited about learning how ticketing worked and how the business could maximise audiences. (In the process, I got a few rock bands mad at me because they didn't like Ticketmaster's business model.[20]) If you look at it in the right spirit, you can find something compelling in just about anything. There are still great mysteries out there that are only vaguely understood: the workings of the human mind; the potential of the Internet; how we might rescue the planet from global warming. You could spend a rewarding lifetime studying any one of them.

[20]Through Ticketmaster fans can find tickets to major events via one website, but many artists have complained about the high fees they charge the fans.

'**Everything is far more interrelated than people realised 20 years ago.** Consider: you can build a whole body from a single cell. In many areas, we're just scratching the surface of understanding; a few, like genomes or decoding, are accelerating a lot faster. Some seem incredibly difficult, like the workings of the human brain. The experts tell me that ocean fisheries work best when they're more controlled, with a preserve – say, a square-mile no-fish zone – where the fish somehow know they're not going to get caught. Creating a preserve builds back the population, and you wind up with more fish than if you had a no-holds-barred open season.

'We're just starting to figure out some of these complex systems. The challenge of global warming, or our need for clean and broadly accessible power, or the threat of a particular microbe – each requires lifetimes of specialisation. I call it "drilling into the orange with a needle". I like to take a different tack. I try to find broad-scale challenges with very specific, concrete goals. At the Allen Institute for Brain Science, we developed a genetic atlas for the mouse brain, and now we're working on the human brain. That's the whole rind of the orange. It's not the end of the process, but it's giving the specialists – the people looking at Alzheimer's, or addiction – a tool with which to accelerate their work. So when they drill *their* needle into the orange, they can go further and more quickly.'

MOVE ONE SPACE FORWARD TO THE NEXT CHAPTER ... OR ROLL THE DICE

Keeping our eyes, ears, noses (and throats) open to what's out there allows our minds to be tuned to new possibilities. In fact, we should never accept just the status quo (however much we love their music) because there are always things to improve upon. Patagonia, the outdoor clothing company with a conscience, has set itself high goals and has been very open about what it can still do better to minimise its environmental impact, while Dutch umbrella-maker SENZ looked at flaws in the design of traditional umbrellas to come up with a new and improved product. It's often hard to imagine what disruptive changes lie lurking just around the corner, but it is guaranteed that change will come. **All industries should learn a lesson from what's happened with the music business and how the revenue model has dramatically changed.** The smart bands have embraced the change and turned it to their advantage. As Paul Allen, the Microsoft co-founder, has shown with his myriad enterprises, the foundation for innovation is having a natural curiosity and constantly absorbing information and ideas. In the next chapter we talk about how coming up with the right version of the problem or question will shape the quality of the creative solutions.

I knew the music business was going pear-shaped in 1985 or 1986 when Jose Menendez was brought in from Hertz Rent-a-Car to run RCA Records in New York. The first I heard of it was when I went to a meeting at his office (our manager had met him once and refused to work with him). I was summoned to meet him and talk about plans for our new Eurythmics' album, called *Be Yourself Tonight*.

I sensed something was wrong as soon as I entered the room, and I had like an instant weird chemical allergic reaction. He was a big man, with a big handshake (which didn't save him later when he and his wife were gunned down by their own children[21]). He said in a booming voice, 'Great album, Stewart!' adding, as he slapped me on the back, 'Sounds just like *Ghostbusters*!' I nearly choked on my gum. Before I could speak he said, 'I've done a deal that's gonna blow you out of the water,' and proceeded to tell me that a major hamburger chain had agreed to make mini Dave and Annie toys and, with every 10 or 20, or whatever number it was, of toys collected you'd get a free album.

I was trying to tell him that Annie was vegetarian (and was also on the cover of that month's *Vegetarian Times* magazine) and was a practising Hare Krishna, but he was very forceful and overbearing and I was soon nudged out of the office. He had artists in and out of there like a revolving door and, as I left, I saw a confused-looking Cyndi Lauper about to be wheeled in. In those 15 minutes I saw the future of the entertainment industry. And it was burger shaped. By 2000 I'd realised that in order for artists and content creators to survive at all, they had to take control of the situation. And so I came up with the idea that we artists should start a 'bank' called, surprisingly enough, First Artists Bank. (I stole the idea from The Farmers Bank.[22]) As you can imagine, trying to round up lots of artists is a bit like trying to saddle a rat, and getting them to talk about finance often seemed about as difficult as selling Bibles in a brothel. Of course, when

[21]Lyle and Erik Menendez shot and killed their parents on 20 August 1989, for which they each received two consecutive life sentences without parole.

[22]The Farmers Bank was one of the first manifestations of a strong move towards economic self-determination.

I got the attention of Deutsche Bank, things started to happen. I pulled together first a meeting in their boardroom in London where Mick Jagger turned up and said loudly, 'This is the first time I've been in a fucking bank in 30 years', and then a meeting in their New York board room at which Stevie Wonder arrived on time – a rarity for Stevie.

Now, when you are standing at the head of a huge boardroom table on the top floor of the biggest European bank in NYC addressing everyone from Quincy Jones to Lou Reed to Stevie Wonder to Jeff Rosen (Bob Dylan's manager), you had better have something to say.

So, I announced that this was the end of the entertainment industry as we knew it.

Michael Philipp, who at the time was on the board of Deutsche Bank[23] and was at the meeting in London as well as hosting the meeting in NYC, recalls, 'When I first met Dave in September 2000, he talked for 12 hours about the impact of digitalisation on the production and distribution of media. As a banker, I didn't know what the hell he was talking about: nor did anyone else. Over the next five years, we all found out.'

Everyone was very interested in what I was saying, but no one was totally convinced by my idea of a bank for artists. There were lots of heated discussions and plenty of puzzled expressions. All the artists knew that I was making some kind of sense but, because I was an artist too, I'm sure they thought, 'Uh-oh, Dave could be nuts but it's hard to tell because we are a bit nuts too.' There were non-artists there, too – a publisher, a record executive, a lawyer representing Dr Dre – and, by the looks on their faces, they were petrified that the lunatics were taking over the asylum.

What I was trying to explain to everyone there was that the Internet can be a good thing, if only we take control. The old business model was to retain control of manufacture and distribution, bamboozle the artists with contracts and then, when the money started rolling in, to hold on to it for as long as possible. And then, finally, months later, when you had to pay the artists what was owed, deduct as much as you could for as many reasons as you can think of (such as a 25 per cent deduction for costs of packaging). Music publishers were basically the equivalent of bad mortgage companies that loan you money at incredibly high interest rates, then, when you have paid off your loan, they still own your property (i.e. your songs).

[23]Michael Philipp then became Chairman and Executive Board Member of Credit Suisse Europe, Middle East and Africa.

Rather than embrace the Internet and find new ways of doing business that reflected consumers' interest in downloading music digitally, the record industry got scared about cannibalising existing sales and missed their opportunity. I think they thought, 'If we keep our heads down it might never happen.' On 15 June 2000 the industry's top executives had gathered for secret talks with Hank Harry, the CEO of Napster, the rogue file-sharing website that had been giving fans access to digital music downloads. They discussed a subscription service for Napster's 38 million users, which would give them the ability to carry on downloading for a monthly flat fee of about $10, revenues to be split between the labels and Napster (but what about the artists?). But the record executives simply couldn't take the final leap and the deal was never done. Napster went bust a year later, but it wasn't for another two years that the industry finally launched a legal, user-friendly service. By then, consumers were too used to other ways of getting the music they wanted.

What I was suggesting with my First Artists Bank (FAB) back in 2000 was that we form a bank that joined all the music rights societies around the world, thereby instantly becoming a publishing company with a transparent payment system so we could see where the money is. Then we'd create digital destinations for artists such as U2, Bob Dylan or Gwen Stefani, and eventually all artists, that are way beyond websites. These would allow them to share, market and monetise their content, merchandise, tickets – and whatever else – to fans on the web and through mobile phones. Payments to the artists would be transparent and swift (seconds rather than the 9 to 27 months it usually takes to get royalty cheques). Our bank would attract customers more interested in getting Glastonbury or Lady Gaga tickets than a subscription to *Reader's Digest*! Gwen Stefani, for instance, in her digital world might include her music (No Doubt and her solo work), her L.A.M.B. clothing range, her co-branded K-Swiss and Hewlett-Packard products, her Harajuku Lovers brand,[24] her music videos, ringtones, digital applications, T-shirts, tickets to her concert – even hotel rooms and travel to the venues. Through her digital world she would get paid through a mixture of à la carte payments, subscriptions and advertising.

One day very soon my idea will be realised. It's taken ten years so far and a lot of meetings but it's finally beginning to happen. I don't think I could have got this far unless

[24] I remember writing songs with Gwen at my Surrey farmhouse and her mentioning she had an idea for a whole Japanese-inspired brand of apparel and fashion accessories.

I had absolute faith in one simple, big audacious idea. I kept asking, 'Why does it have to be this way?' over and over again. I didn't see why I had to follow the rules if they no longer made sense. Children do this too; they constantly question us adults about why the world is the way it is and sometimes the answer, 'Just because', isn't enough. The entertainment industry needed to change and I could see a straightforward (I didn't say an easy) way to change it. As they say, 'necessity is the mother of invention', and in this labour the birth has been long overdue.

Here is a mind map of our vision for FAB[25]

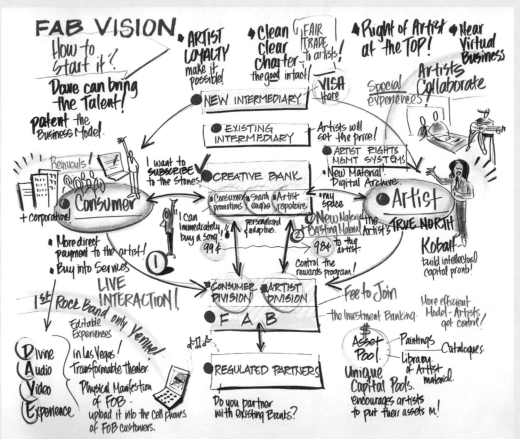

[25]It's just one slide of a whole bunch we did as we worked on the concept, and involved contributions from then CEO of Visa international, Christopher Rodrigues, Andy Law, Frank Nuovo and John Kao who was hosting the session.

A B C D E F G H I J

10 9 8 7 6 5 4 3 2 1

A B C D E F G H I J

Instructions

1. Answer 12 questions about familiar things to find where the hidden treasure is buried.
2. The answers you choose will determine where on the circular path you move (it's like the dial of a safe).
3. After 12 moves you will find yourself at one of the 10 points.
4. Go to its corresponding star on the map to find where the treasure is buried.
5. Look at its coordinates and check at the back of the book to see if you were right!

START

BOARD GAME: SCAVENGERS

How it works: There is a treasure trove of ideas out there just waiting to be discovered, it's just a matter of keeping our wits about us. If we keep our eyes open we might be able to see things that others don't notice or just take for granted without ever really thinking about them.

How to play: From the start point on the map players move along the circular path and answer questions that test their powers of observation. Each one has two possible answers – one right and one wrong – and depending which one they choose, the players move a marker a certain number of spaces clockwise or anticlockwise (markers can be a coin or anything else to mark the space on the circle). Remember that where the marker is at any stage of the game has nothing to do with which question you're answering – for instance, you could be on question number 8 and have your marker at number 5 (and no, that's not a clue). After answering the 12 questions, each time moving their markers clockwise or anticlockwise as directed, players will find themselves at one of the 10 points on the circle. This will take them to the 'X' where the treasure is buried. It's like a giant safe and players are looking for the secret code!

How to win: Once they have arrived at what they think is the right X, players determine what are its coordinates, then check to see if they were right by looking at page 234 where they can also see the correct answers to each question. Good luck!

The questions:

One: How many times does the letter F appear in the sentence below?

'When I visited Phil, finches of Japan were flying around the flourishing bonsai placed on the left of the lounge's entry.'

5 = 2 spaces clockwise,
6 = 2 spaces anticlockwise

Two: On a standard traffic light is the green light at the top or bottom?

TOP = 4 spaces clockwise,
BOTTOM = 4 spaces anticlockwise

Three: How many curves are there on a paper clip?

3 CURVES = 1 space clockwise,
4 CURVES = 1 space anticlockwise

Four: In which hand is the Statue of Liberty's torch?

RIGHT HAND = 5 spaces clockwise,
LEFT HAND = 5 spaces anticlockwise

Five: Which way do fans rotate?

CLOCKWISE = 8 spaces clockwise,
ANTICLOCKWISE = 8 spaces anticlockwise

Six: How many sides are there on a standard pencil?

6 SIDES = 3 spaces clockwise,
8 SIDES = 3 spaces anticlockwise

Seven: Do books have even-numbered pages on the right or left side?

LEFT SIDE = 7 spaces clockwise,
RIGHT SIDE = 7 spaces anticlockwise

Eight: On the American flag is the top stripe red or white?

WHITE = 3 spaces clockwise,
RED = 3 spaces anticlockwise

Nine: On a typical phone keypad which of these number keys has no letters on it?

1 = 2 spaces clockwise,
9 = 2 spaces anticlockwise

Ten: When you walk does your right arm swing with your right or left leg?

LEFT = 1 space clockwise,
RIGHT = 1 space anticlockwise

Eleven: Which card in a pack of playing cards carries the manufacturer's trademark?

JOKER = move 2 spaces clockwise,
ACE OF SPADES = move 2 spaces anticlockwise

Twelve: How many differences are there between these two pictures?

4 = move 9 spaces clockwise,
5 = move 9 spaces anticlockwise

Check out our website, **www.businessplayground.com**, for more scavenger games.

CHAPTER FOUR

THE ANSWER IS IN THE QUESTION

Why getting the best answer means asking the right questions in the first place.

When Jorma Ollila joined Nokia in the mid 1980s, the giant Finnish corporation made toilet paper and wellies. Nokia Corporation was the result of a merger between a paper company, a rubber goods company and a cable company.[2] Ollila became the CEO in 1992 and when he took over he asked, 'What business should Nokia be in?' His answer was mobile communications and, against the wishes of many Nokia shareholders, executives and employees, over the next few years he sold off all the assets not aligned to this new focus and helped transform the company's fortunes (profits increasing five-fold between 1993, before the changes kicked in, and 1999), and with it the Finnish economy. Nokia is now the biggest mobile-phone manufacturer in the world and has a 40 per cent share of all handsets sold. Not a rubber boot in sight. And *now* Nokia has asked itself that question again, what business should they be in, and the answer is different once more. Nokia is currently transforming itself into a media company by offering music, games and applications through its phones, and plans to be the world's biggest entertainment network.

The questions we ask shape the answers we get, and posing the right question is an art in itself. Before we unleash our creative energy (and our time, money and resources) on finding creative solutions to a problem, we need to question the assumptions we're making about the problem we're trying to solve. Is it in fact the *right* problem in the first

[1]Why did no-one ask for their name?

[2]This sounds like the beginning of a joke …

place, or are we basing it on a bunch of flimsy assumptions? When Albert Einstein got home from school his mother asked him not what grades he got, but whether he had asked any good questions. Jorma Ollila of Nokia didn't focus on how to increase sales of toilet paper, even though Nokia had started life in 1865 as a lumber mill; he questioned the assumption that Nokia needed to have all those diverse and unrelated businesses to survive. Someone that one of us used to work with was apt to say, '"Assume" makes an "ass" out of "u" and "me".' A little irritating when you've heard it a few times, but you get the point: **it's important to examine each assumption we're making to see if it actually holds up to scrutiny.**

What if, for instance, we turn an assumption on its head by looking at its exact opposite? Does it make a real difference? If so, keep it in, if not, you might want to dump it. To illustrate how different assumptions can change a problem we'll use one dear to our hearts: the traffic congestion in Los Angeles.[3] The average annual delay per road user in Los Angeles stands (mostly stationary) at 93 hours.[4] If a problem we are trying to solve is how to reduce traffic congestion in LA, what sort of assumptions are we making, and do they pass the sniff test? The assumptions include:

- **There's too much traffic in LA.**
- **People don't like being stuck in traffic.**
- **Congestion slows things down.**
- **It's a bad thing to have congestion.**
- **People need cars to get around.**
- **People need to travel around LA.**

[3]The point of this example is not actually to solve the problem of traffic congestion – there are a million worthy efforts dedicated to that – it's just to illustrate how to think through a problem that you should be able to relate to.

[4]Data from 'Commuting in America', Alan Pisarski, *Transportation Research Board*, 2006.

Duh, we might think – those all look blindingly obviously true. Maybe so, but let's just hold our horses for a minute and take a closer look at these assumptions. For instance, the first one, *There's too much traffic in LA*, begs the questions what is *too much* and, *compared to what* exactly? And how about the second one, *People don't like being stuck in traffic*? Some people might love being stuck in traffic and maybe they've got used to that time alone in their cars drinking coffee, making calls and shaving/applying lipstick/both at the same time.[5] The third one, *Congestion slows things down*, seems solid, as does the fourth, *It's a bad thing to have congestion*. But the fifth assumption, *People need cars to get around*? Nah, that's baloney.

People clearly don't need cars to get around

– they have legs (even the people in LA), bicycles, buses (sort of) and if you look really, really hard, the occasional train. Of course, if you've spent any time in Los Angeles you'll know these alternatives don't make much sense unless you're travelling just a couple of miles, and even then you take your life in your own hands (or someone else's hands if they're applying lipstick and shaving while driving). But there definitely are alternatives; they just might need a little working on.

And the last assumption, *People need to travel around LA*, is sort of true in that they need to get to work and go to the shops to buy food and stuff, but many of the journeys are for non-essential things like going out to eat, or going to a movie, or going to the beach. We don't want to party-poopers here … we're just saying.

Is it perhaps better to find ways to reduce the need to travel around LA in the first place, rather than make travel easier? As anyone who has spent time in LA knows, it is very spread out, it's

---

[5]In 2003 a woman from Ohio was fined for breastfeeding her 1-year-old baby while driving (the mother, not the baby). In 2009, a Chinese lorry driver was fined for taking a shower while driving his lorry along the Jinyi expressway. He had a sprinkler system rigged above his head while his wife in the passenger seat held a plastic sheet up to protect the cab's instruments.

actually not one city but 88 of them, and maybe transportation as a whole is the problem – whether that's by bus, train or car – and by trying to switch people to public transport we'd just be dealing with the effect of the problem rather than its cause. Being transported around is dangerous, for instance, and it uses up valuable fuels, produces dirty emissions, takes up precious time and costs money. So, rather than assume people need to travel around Los Angeles, we could choose to tackle a different problem altogether, namely how to get people to travel around LA less. This version of the problem suggests a need for ideas that are not solutions for better public transportation and other ways for making getting around easier, but instead for solutions for ways to **encourage people to work from home and improve local services so they don't have to travel around much at all.** Of course, that wouldn't satisfy the people who like being stuck in traffic drinking coffee, shaving and putting on lipstick – but maybe that's OK.

If we decide the best problem to solve is how to get people to use their cars less,

the ideas might include encouraging people to work from home more or penalising their unnecessary use of cars through taxes and fees, as Mayor Ken Livingstone did in London,[6] or even by bribing commuters to leave their cars at home. In 2006 the city of Seoul, South Korea, launched their 'No-Driving Day' scheme in which drivers are given incentives to leave their cars at home for one day every week. Provided by public organisations and private companies, the incentives include discounts on auto tax, cheaper petrol, free parking and free car washes. Drivers stick e-tags (using Radio Frequency Identification Technology, or RDIF) on their windscreens so the city can monitor car usage and see if they are eligible for the discounts and freebies. It's estimated the scheme keeps two million cars off the road each year, reducing traffic volume by 3.7 per cent, reducing carbon emissions by two million tons and saving $50 million a year in fuel costs.[7]

[6]The congestion charge was introduced in London by then Mayor of London, Ken Livingstone, in February 2003.

[7]www.c40cities.org/bestpractices/transport/seoul_driving.jsp

SPLITTING THE CHERRY

Another way to look at a problem is to split it up into smaller chunks and explore some of those as separate problems. We start by writing the problem in its simplest form, such as 'traffic sucks', and then split that problem into two pieces.

Now we split each of those cherries up into two more chunks. For example, two big problems with drivers is that they don't pay attention (we, of course, are great drivers, it's just those *other* drivers that are so bad), and there are just too many of them blocking our way. And two big issues for roads is that there aren't enough of the bloody things and, anyway, they're closed half the time.

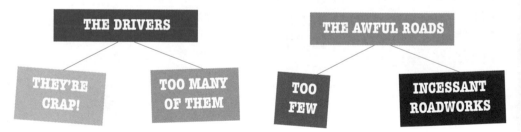

We carry on splitting up the cherry until we can't do it any more and end up with a tree diagram (a cherry tree!) of all the individual problems that make up the bigger problem. From these we can decide which ones to focus on.

(Just a thought, but how about redirecting all the really crap drivers into the holes made for the road works?)

SOMETHING FISHY

Try not to be put off by the size of the problem, however stinky it might seem at first, because it can almost always be broken up into smaller, more manageable chunks. Think of it as a fish bone.

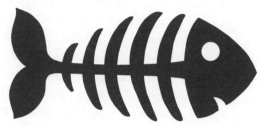

Using a technique developed by a Japanese dude named Kaoru Ishikawa – who in the 1960s developed the fishbone as a process to manage work in the Kawasaki shipyards – can help us break up the big problem. First, by stating it as simply as possible and writing it on our fish head, and then on the bones that make up the skeleton putting down the things that are the key factors. When we have stuck in every one we can think of and written them on the fish bones, we then start to think through possible ways to address them, one bone at a time. It's a bit like the cherry-splitting technique, but where the cherries taste like cod.

The Mazda MX-5 car, also known as the Miata, was developed using Ishikawa's fishbone method. According to the *Guinness Book of World Records*, the MX-5 is the most popular sports car ever built. Designers in California and Japan started with a design credo called 人馬一体, or *jinba ittai*, which translates roughly as 'rider and horse as one'. It was all about driving fun – that wind-in-the-hair driving experience you get when riding a horse (or maybe from blow-drying your hair). They then broke the design credo into five separate elements that together would deliver the car they were looking for: it needed to be compact and lightweight while still safe; have a cockpit big enough for two normal-sized adults; an engine placement that gave 50:50 weight redistribution across the front and rear of the car; all four wheels evenly used on the road to enhance stability and performance; and lastly, a good connection between the engine and rear differential so it was very responsive to pressure on the throttle.

The first MX-5 galloped off the production line in February 1989 and, two decades and 900,000 sales later, the MX-5 had gone through three generations of design, each one staying true to the five core design principles outlined in their original fishbone diagram. Ah so.

I had been working on the musical *GHOST* with the Tony-Award-winning stage director Matthew Warchus.[8] As you can imagine, putting on a stage musical is a massive undertaking for all concerned and is a nightmare of logistics. The director has to consult the set designer, the special effects expert, the lighting engineer, the actors and the actresses, etc., on every decision because of timing and practicality issues. And, of course, let's not forget the music and lyrics, which have to not only help tell the story but often do so in 'timed by the stopwatch' organised sections, so that the music and stagecraft work seamlessly hand-in-hand with sets that are moving and have actors and actresses leaping around them.

When a problem appears it can be overwhelming for us mere mortals to fathom out how to fix it, as one thing affects everything else. Fortunately, we have Matthew, who is not normal! Matthew is a classic example of someone who uses 'The Answer Is The Question' method of decision-making. He also uses the method of breaking everything down into small pieces like Kaoru Ishikawa did. In fact, one very drunken night in 'The Hospital' (not a medical hospital but the creative members club I founded with Paul Allen) Matthew broke down the whole musical into what looked like a block diagram (see picture) on The Hospital Club's 'Today's Specials' menu board from the bar. Each block represented a scene and had a colour border, and each colour that was repeated in another block meant those scenes were connected and had a musical thread running through them.

This simple way of standing back and looking at the whole musical helped us solve many issues and brought about interesting Big Questions, such as: What is the musical really about? We all had our own ideas but even Bruce Joel Rubin, the writer of the original film screenplay who was working with us, was amazed at how Matthew simplified the whole show in five minutes in

[8]Among many other accolades, Matthew has won the Globe's Most Promising Newcomer Award for Shakespeare's *Much Ado About Nothing* and has won the *Evening Standard* Best Director Award; was nominated for the Olivier Award for Shakespeare's *Henry V* and Ben Jonson's *Volpone*; won the Drama Desk Award for Best Director of a Play for his production of Alan Ayckbourn's trilogy of plays, *The Norman Conquests* at London's Old Vic Theatre; and competed against himself – and won – in the Best Director of a Play category in the 2009 Tony Awards.

front of us after several vodka martinis and a full-bodied red wine!

Matthew told Business Playground in an interview: 'My job is storytelling, and scripts are written in linear form or they are presented in a linear form – you read them from the first page to the last – and when an audience then watches a story, they receive it in a linear sequence. But, the effect the story has on an audience is not achieved through a linear sequence. The emotional effect of the story is achieved by patterns, and so only by creating a chart can you start to look at what the patterns are in the story, or what patterns you want to emphasise, or what patterns you want to add to the story. Those little "mirrors" and "reflections" and "echoes" that recur in the story – a park bench and the things that take place there, a piece of music that keeps coming back in a musical, or a phrase like "ditto" in the film *Ghost* – all these little things make the pattern that creates the emotion in a story.'

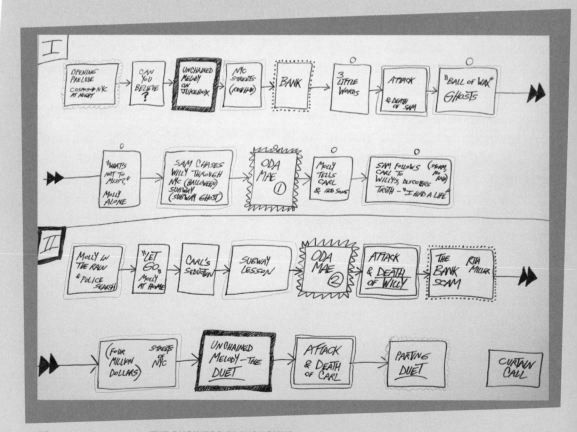

DIFFERENT STROKES

In crafting a problem, looking at it from different points of view can help. **We in our own little worlds might see it in one way, but others will almost certainly see it in other ways; and stepping into their shoes for a while can help us reframe the problem so we can decide what is the best question to ask.** With the traffic congestion conundrum, for instance, if you are the mayor of the city you might have a different way of looking at it than if you are the police chief, an environmentalist or a regular commuter. All might agree that the problem is a bad one that needs to be solved, but exactly *why* it needs to be solved will vary depending on viewpoint.

The mayor might be most concerned that too much time is lost through bad traffic, which is affecting businesses throughout the city, and would like to see office workers in LA having to spend less of their day stuck in cars. The police chief probably cares less about productivity (and getting votes from business leaders) and more that the sheer volume of traffic is a major cause of accidents and fatalities, and so a drain on police resources. The environmentalist hates the traffic because exhaust fumes are poisoning the atmosphere. And commuters don't like the congestion because it takes up too much time and is stressful. From which perspective we look at the problem will help us prioritise the ingredients required to achieve the best solution. If the time commuters spend travelling to work is a really important consideration, for instance, and public transport is being considered as a solution, then encouraging people to travel by clean, natural, gas-powered buses – a great solution from an environmental point of view – might *not* be the best answer, as buses make so many stops and therefore tend to be slower than cars.

'Different Strokes' is a good group exercise to help define the problem. If there's a small team of people working on an innovation project, you can assign roles for each one of them. Make it fun by giving them names and even finding some props to help get them into character. (It's also a good technique to use when you have what you think is a good solution to a problem, or a great idea for an innovation and need to get buy-in from stakeholders.) **Again, putting yourself in the shoes of other people – people with different agendas – can help you see what the challenges in getting them to endorse it might be.** Just make sure they have clean socks on. You can take account of their concerns before they've even told you, and if you can deal with them you have a way better chance of seeing your idea happen.

MOVE ONE SPACE FORWARD TO THE NEXT CHAPTER ... OR ROLL THE DICE

If we get the problem right in the first place we have a better chance of finding the best solution. To start with we need to do a bit of navel-gazing as we examine all the assumptions we're making about a situation, and then get rid of all of the ones that don't hold true. Nokia questioned some very fundamental assumptions about its disparate businesses before deciding to change direction to mobiles, eventually becoming the biggest mobile manufacturer in the world, and more recently deciding to shift again by focusing its efforts on becoming a media distribution company. Again, the answer is often in the question and if we ask the right question we will more likely get the right answers. **How we frame a problem will lead to very different creative solutions and so it's worth working through the various versions of the problem we want to solve.** We used the example of traffic congestion to see how reframing it would send us in a different direction creatively. Sometimes breaking up bigger problems into smaller pieces is the way to go when the problem just seems too big to tackle, a technique that has been used successfully in shipyards, car design, and for stage productions. In the next chapter we show how, for our creative abilities to do their work properly, they need a little breathing room. OK, now open wide, say, 'Ah ...'

Instructions

1. Decide on a problem you want to solve and phrase it 'How can we ...?'
2. Throw a die to determine a type of question to ask yourself about the problem.
   1 = How?
   2 = Why?
   3 = Which?
   4 = When?
   5 = Who?
   6 = What?
3. When you reach the last space, use what you've discovered from your answers to rewrite the problem 'How can we ...?'
4. This new version of the problem will be better than the one you started with!

HOW CAN WE ...?

BOARD GAME: WHAT'S YOUR PROBLEM?

How it works: Working out the right business problem to solve is a bit like putting a band together. It takes patience and practice, but when you get it right you can make some sweet, sweet music. If you ask a question like 'How do we sell more of our music?', for instance, you'll likely end up with a very different answer compared to one like 'How do we make money from our music?' The first one assumes that selling music is the best way to make money from selling music, but the second one doesn't.

How to play: Players start by writing down a business problem as a question starting with: How can we ...? They then ask themselves a series of questions about the problem to get it to a more insightful version. The end result should be simple and clear. (As German abstract expressionist painter, Hans Hoffman, said, 'The ability to simplify means to eliminate the unnecessary so that the necessary may speak.' He could have just said 'Keep it simple, stupid' instead, but, oh well, never mind.) Players move down each step by throwing a die and, depending on the number that comes up, ask themselves a different question about the problem they're trying to solve:

1 = HOW?
2 = WHY?
3 = WHICH?
4 = WHEN?
5 = WHO?
6 = WHAT?

Example: Say you have a band and your problem is 'How can we sell more music?', you throw a 6, a WHAT question, and so ask yourself, 'WHAT are the barriers to selling more music?' You come up with a few answers such as, fewer people are buying music nowadays; the economy stinks; not enough people know about us; or, our music sucks. Next you throw a 2 and so you ask yourself, 'WHY are people spending less on buying music?' Your answer is that people can get it for free online. Now you throw a 4 and ask yourself 'WHEN do people spend money on music?' The answers might be when they buy special editions with all sorts of extra content or when they're seeing live gigs. Next you throw a 1 and choose to rephrase the problem as: 'HOW do we make the stuff we sell better than the versions people can get for free?' Now you throw a 5 and ask yourself 'WHO is it that pays to get extra content when they can get the music for free elsewhere?' Your answer might be die-hard fans.

And so on. When we hit the last space we can write up the problem in a new way, using the insights gathered throughout the game. It might be something like, 'How can we make our music releases special enough that die-hard fans will pay good money to buy them?' Now that's a more tangible problem to crack. But, depending on our previous answers, we might instead have chosen a different reframing of the problem. For instance, one around not trying to sell music but concentrating our efforts on live gigs to earn money and using the recorded music as a promotional tool for them, and that will lead to a whole different set of solutions around finding third-party sponsors (see Chapter 3).

How to win: Find the best way to frame a problem and everyone's a winner, baby!

CHAPTER FIVE

LEFT BRAIN, MEET MR RIGHT

**Helping the two halves
of our brains work together.**

DRIVEN TO DISTRACTION[1]

Now the real fun starts. Once we've defined what the problem is we can begin to unleash our creative powers to solve it. There are some powerful techniques to use, beyond just staring into space or taking a hot bath waiting for that 'Eureka!' moment,[2] although it has to be said just staring into space or taking a hot bath can actually work (as can having a shower, or doing some exercise, or going on a bus). **Once the brain has been given a clear problem to work on, doing something completely different lets it stew for a while and do its voodoo.** Organic chemist Friedrich August Kekulé was

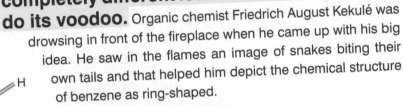

drowsing in front of the fireplace when he came up with his big idea. He saw in the flames an image of snakes biting their own tails and that helped him depict the chemical structure of benzene as ring-shaped.

Mathematician Henri Poincaré wrote[3] about his own experience of a creative solution popping up when he was distracted doing something completely unrelated: 'I turned my attention to the study of some arithmetical questions apparently without much success and without a suspicion of any connection with my preceding researches. Disgusted with my failure, I went to spend a few days at the seaside, and thought of something else. One morning, walking on the bluff, the idea came to me ... that the arithmetic transformations of indeterminate ternary quadratic forms were identical to those of non-Euclidian geometry.'

[1]There isn't any place called Distraction anywhere that we could find, which seems like a wasted opportunity for some funny dialogue.

[2]As Archimedes did when wallowing in the bath, he suddenly came up with the idea for how to measure the volume of an irregular object. He ran naked through the streets of Syracuse shouting 'Eureka!'. We don't know what the shocked citizens of Syracuse shouted back.

[3]*The Mathematician's Mind: The Psychology of Invention in the Mathematical Field*, J. Hadamard, Princeton University Press, 1945.

(Personally, we thought it was obvious that arithmetic transformations of indeterminate ternary quadratic forms are identical to those of non-Euclidian geometry, and are surprised Henri hadn't realised that straight away.)

The period of unconscious thought in which the brain is not focusing on the problem at hand is known as *incubation*, and it's often during this time that the solution pops up. You're in the gym sweating away on a machine thinking about how to keep from collapsing and embarrassing yourself in front of everyone when, WHAM!, from nowhere you come up with an idea for solving the problem you've been working on for days. You're so surprised that you fall off the machine and embarrass yourself anyway, but you don't care because you have the answer.

Matthew Warchus told Business Playground how he needs mental space when he's trying to solve problems creatively: 'I'm in a very strange position when I work with an assistant director. I find it quite difficult when I work with an assistant because I like collaborating – it's obviously my job to collaborate – but the only way I can work with assistants is if I tell them when they start with me, "Feel free to speak and comment, and things like that, follow me round, come to the meetings and all that. All I ask is that if I'm stuck don't help me. If things are going along really well then chip in, say what you want, but if I'm stuck don't say anything, because being stuck comes just before having a really brilliant idea." To me that's when having really special ideas come, just after being stuck. I think it's the magic moment creatively when you get a room full of people who are all stuck. I like that, it's a good sign.'

Creativity involves making connections between things that didn't previously appear to be connected. In 1913 Poincaré[4] wrote: 'To create consists of making new combinations of associative elements which are useful ... the most fertile will often be those formed of elements drawn from domains which are far apart.' And recent research proves that being distracted from a creative challenge for a while can bear fruit (mainly plums, but mangoes too sometimes). In one study[5] undergraduates studying (or whatever students do) at the University of Amsterdam were each given a creative problem to solve, then they were either given three minutes to think it through before giving their answers, or given another task to do for the three minutes to distract them, or they were asked to come up with their ideas right away.

They had various creative tasks to perform: to create new names for pastas, having been given examples of some made-up names to help them (all of the examples happened to end with the letter 'i' – you'll see where this is going if you hang around a bit); come up with names of Dutch places starting with the letter 'A' (we can think of just one,[6] but the tests were conducted in the Netherlands so our guess is these people were better at it than us); to come up with ideas for some creative uses a brick (don't get us started).

Now remember that some of the students were distracted by another task before giving their answers. Those students randomly allocated to this *distracted group*, immediately having been given their creative task were given another, but this time a non-creative task, one designed to occupy their *conscious thoughts*. A circle appeared on their computer screens in a random place and they had to track it with their computer mouse and sometimes, we presume

[4]*The Foundations of Science*, H. Poincaré, The Science Press, 1913.

[5]'Where Creativity Resides: The Generative Power of Unconscious Thought', A. Dijksterhuis and T. Meurs, *Consciousness and Cognition*, 2006.

[6]Alkmaar. Did you think we were going to say Amsterdam? Nah.

just to mess with their heads, the circle would change colour and they (who probably by now thought they were in some weird, Dutch drug-induced haze) had to click the space bar as fast as possible until the circle disappeared. Then a new one would appear, and so on for three minutes. The people in the other two groups seem to have got off relatively lightly, and either had to give answers straight off the bat for their creative tasks or were given three minutes to think up ideas first.

Results from the three experiments varied for the three groups. Ignoring the fact that we've just told you that the *distracted group* performed better, you might logically think that being give time to focus on the problem would help. But, oh no, that's not what happened at all. For instance, the distracted group generated more pasta names that did not end with an 'i' and their pasta names were more original than the those of the other group, who had created pasta names more similar to the ones given in the examples (that's where *that* was going). The distracted folks came up with more Dutch villages rather than the obvious big cities and towns when compared to their less-distracted brethren, and again the solutions they generated were less obvious. And, you guessed it, the distracted group generated more creative suggestions for what to do with a brick (such as, and we're guessing here, 'Throw it at the middle of the moving circle on the computer screen!').

How does one explain these results? As the Dutch researchers conclude, in way better English than most English-speaking natives would use, **'Whereas conscious thought stays firmly under the searchlight, unconscious thought ventures out to the dark and dusty nooks and crannies of the mind.'** The weird circle-tracking task had occupied their conscious thoughts, so freeing up their unconscious to do some nifty creative work. It's like letting a dog off the lead in a park. If you let the creative part of your brain go run around for a while (the dog), without being restricted by the more rigorous conscious thought (the lead), it will come back with lots of interesting ideas (in this analogy: sticks, balls and dead birds).

Monsieur Poincaré, our French mathematician friend, believed that the products of unconscious thought often do not enter the conscious mind right away, but pop up in there later unexpectedly. We've all experienced the feeling that there's *something there*, some interesting idea or solution that we can't quite put into words yet. In fact,[7] there's a two-step process going on. In the first, unconscious thought goes to work looking for creative solutions by exploring the dark and dusty nooks and crannies, and in the second, the solutions are transferred across to conscious thought.

The task often used in research on creativity is known as the Remote Association Test (RAT) because it tasks people with finding remote associations between things. This fits nicely with the Frenchman's description of creativity. In one form of RAT, for instance, people are given three words and they need to come up with a fourth that fits with each of them. Ready to try one? Cheese – Ocean – Sky.

Quickly … quickly …

The answer is *blue*. As in *blue cheese*, *blue ocean* and *blue sky*. Here are a few more to play around with. The answers are at the end of the chapter (see page 102), but the last few are pretty tricky so don't be surprised if you don't get them all.

[7]'The Merits of Unconscious Thought in Creativity', Cheh-Bo Zhong, Ap Dijksterhuis and Adam Galinsky, *Psychological Science*, 2008.

Light – Birthday – Stick

Cross – Rain – Tie

Boot – Summer – Ground

Manners – Round – Tennis

Health – Taker – Less

Off – Trumpet – Atomic

Carpet – Alert – Ink

Test – Runner – Map

Man – Glue – Star

Here are the trickier ones …

Stick – Maker – Point

Foot – Collection – Out

Line – Fruit – Drunk

Mate – Shoes – Total

Land – Hand – House

Bump – Throat – Sum

Problems like these can be solved in one of two ways: either by trial and error, an analytical process whereby we consciously go through word combinations to see if one of them fits (for the last one in the list you might have started with 'Off' to make 'Castoff' and tried it with the other two words before realising that wouldn't work), or solve the problem through insight. **There's an 'A-ha!' moment when the answer arrives from your subconscious. That's the creative bit at work.** And it's funny, but that 'A-ha!' feeling is how people almost always describe it (unless you're Greek, in which case 'Eureka' is the more usual cry). So when researchers want to find out if someone got the answer through analysis or insight, they ask them to say whether or not they got that 'A-ha!' feeling when they found the solution, and their answer tells the researchers which method of problem-solving was used.

It turns out that the brain actually *prepares* itself to come up with an insight when it's using the insight method even before it's solved the problem. It's limbering itself up to be creative. Researchers[8] put people in brain-scanning machines and used electroencephalography (EEG) and functional magnetic resonance imaging (fMRI) to look at their neural activity during problem-solving tasks. Subjects were given RAT problems to solve and told to press a button when they had the answer that indicated whether they had solved it with or without insight. Did they get the 'A-ha!' feeling or not? Well, did they? If the problem was solved with insight then the brain activity looked different *even before* they came up with the answer. The brain was preparing itself for going down the 'A-ha' route.

But more than that, brain activity for the 'A-ha' method compared to the analytical one was different, not just before the problem was solved, but, wait for it, even *before the problem was given to them*. Even before they were given the problem, data from the scans showed that people's brains had decided which method to use – insight or analysis. The different people tested in the study didn't just use one or the other method to solve the problems, each person used both insight and analysis to solve the problems at different times and switched between the two methods. Perhaps they were trying a different approach to see which one was most effective, or maybe giving one part of their brain a rest.

Phew. I think you need a break to digest all this. Have a cuppa and then come back to us. We'll still be here.

[8]'The Prepared Mind: Neural Activity Prior to Problem Presentation Predicts Subsequent Solution by Sudden Insight', John Kounios, Jennifer L. Frymiare, Edward M. Bowden, Jessica I. Fleck, Karuna Subramaniam, Todd B. Parrish and Mark Jung-Beeman, *Psychological Science*, 2006.

I get tons of emails from people asking for some creative advice and, whenever possible, I give them free ideas to get their wheels turning. In the next few chapters are examples of some typical email exchanges.

20 August 2009

Evening Dave,

It was good to hear you speak at the Conference in Yorkshire and I recollect your offer for people to contact you. With this in mind I am wondering if you have any advice for a family bicycle shop who also hand-builds custom steel bicycle framesets on the premises? How do we keep our customers loyal, grow our customer base and keep customers coming into the shop rather than purchasing through the Internet? Any thoughts? My husband and I have owned the business since 2000, when the previous owner retired to Canada age 80, and the business was established in 1946 so seen lots of changes, and Paul, MD, has worked in the business around 18 years.

Many thanks.
Yours in cycling,
Sandra Corcoran, Director, Pennine Cycles

Dear Sandra,

I would suggest getting an old-fashioned Italian espresso or cappuccino machine, creating a coffee-club type atmosphere in a small area where people can hang around while they wait. Put a mini library all about cycling and adventure, old and new books, ask customers to swap cycling stories on your website and print them each week or put them on the wall in the coffee area. Customers stay loyal and keep coming back to a place that has personality and a feeling that the owners care and want them there, and it's good fun for you too. Give the different coffee names like 'Wheels on Fire', or 'First-gear Espresso'. Make it humourous. Create outings with the coffee-club clientele and take photos of the outings and place them on the web and in the finished coffee corner. Start a Twitter about cycling, coffee, music and romance. Make cycling and meeting people fun and it could lead to relationships that last.

Dave

Evening Dave,

Lovely ideas. Appreciate you getting back to me. We do hand-built sexy bikes as well as selling Italian sexy bicycles and we are passionate about cycling and our business so it all fits in nicely. One of our first bicycles was named 'Marilyn' after Marilyn Monroe in the 50s. We do offer coffee to our customers, we just need to make more space and get the cappuccino machine in operation now. Love the coffee titles!! Paul has lots of books on cycling so we need to set them up at the shop. Hand-built Pennine bicycles have a following worldwide too. A Pennine is on its way to California in September and a guy from near San Francisco is wanting to refurb a Pennine and needs some Pennine decals. It is a fun business to be in and my husband says it's the best job ever and I am sure you feel the same.

Happy days.

Yours in cycling,
Sandra

SWITCHING GEARS

OK, ready? So, to sum up, what going over these scientific studies has told us is this: first, when we have a creative problem to solve and we turn our minds to something else for a while, the distraction can actually *help* us solve it. Second, people often solve problems through sudden insight and get an 'A-ha' feeling when they do so. In fact, our brains can switch between using insight or the analytical method of problem solving and do so pretty frequently. Third, the brain spontaneously switches between methods, perhaps to give its various bits and pieces a rest.

So far, so good. Now, while people can generally switch from one mode to another to solve problems like these, certain people are predisposed to solve them through the insight method. They veer towards finding those 'A-has'. Using the same sort of techniques (i.e. RAT, EEG and fMRI, if you want the acronyms) scientists[9] looked at resting brain activity to see how it differed among people, and found that activity in certain parts of the right hemisphere of the brain is higher for people who tend to solve the problems using insight. That's interesting; it means that some folks use insight to solve creative problems more than others and their brains are getting into gear to do so ahead of time. Hmm.

So, are certain people more creative than others?

No doubt,[10] but as the research shows, all of us have the ability to switch into creative mode to solve problems, we just need to train our brains to think that way so it gets used to doing it. **As Louis Pasteur (man, these French thinkers were smart) said: 'Chance favours only the prepared mind.'** He believed preparation facilitates insight and, while he was specifically referring to the need to gather information (see the interview with Paul Allen in Chapter 3), we think it also applies to the preparation of our brains to think creatively. That's what we're going to look at next: what stimulates our brains to think more creatively.

[9]'The Origins of Insight in Resting-State Brain Activity', John Kounios, Jessica I. Fleck, Deborah L. Green, Lisa Payne, Jennifer L. Stevenson, Edward M. Bowden and Mark Jung-Beeman, *Neuropsychologia*, 2007.

[10]In fact, Einstein's brain was physically different from most other brains. When Einstein died his brain was dissected into 240 blocks, nearly all of which were lost (they should have sent them by registered post), though luckily not all of them were. One piece remained and, 30 years later, the chunk that's known as 'Brodmann's Area 39' was analysed by Dr Marian C. Diamond and colleagues who found that it contained a higher proportion of *glial* cells versus neurons when compared to brains of control subjects.

Hello Dave,

My company is a fairly small but fast-growing manufacturer of products that provide indoor air quality into homes. Basically, we are on a mission to improve the health and wellbeing of people by delivering fresh, filtered air into homes. According to the American College of Allergists, 50 per cent of the world's illnesses are attributed to poor indoor air, which causes respiratory illnesses, headaches, fatigue, cot deaths, and in some cases stress and depression. And the problem is getting worse as we seal our properties up to save energy. The air we deliver into homes is as fresh and clean as the air found in the Amazon Rainforest (you will never see a monkey using an inhaler*). This fresh filtered air we deliver promotes good health and wellbeing, reduces illnesses and actually improves performance. There is a huge worldwide potential for our products in what is basically an untapped market and after seeing you at Harrogate last month I thought I would have nothing to lose in emailing you. I was wondering if you were prepared to talk to me to see if we can tap into your creativity and come up with a message to the mass market which will create a demand for fresh, clean, oxygenated air. It would be great to hear from you with any thoughts.

Nick Heaton
Managing Director, EnviroVent

* Our products literally are tested on animals!

Dear Nick,

'EnviroVent' is quite a tough name to sell yet I can see that the business could be huge. Selling the idea of breathing clean air and avoiding various illnesses should not be tough and if you can scale up fast enough to meet demand then it may be worth investing in a visual way that gets across your message using every viral trick in the book and the web as a platform. Make an electronic email-able Flash version of a short film of around 60 seconds that tells the story (have a song like *All You Need is the Air That You Breathe* as the soundtrack) and make it a little like an animated film you see on Virgin Airlines about safety on board (even though it's serious, it has some lighthearted humourous aspect to it). There are young Flash animators that can do this with your guidance on their laptop very cheaply and to save $$$ you could write a simple song about 'fresh clean air' and hire a music programmer to create a track and get a session singer to sing it, and then you own it! If you can afford it you could make little 60-second webisodes with Flash animation that explains all the reasons to use your product, having the song as a thread through it. If it's fun and informational and at the end says 'brought to you by EnviroVent' then it can be seeded on blogs, etc., all over the world. Also start Twittering asap about the air we breathe and all the concerns about it with hundreds of tags.

Dave

TUNING UP TO BE CREATIVE ... MUSIC PLEASE, MAESTRO

You're not going to be particularly surprised by this, especially given that one of the authors of this book is a musician and the other likes to whistle, but there is a strong link between musical ability and creative ability. But don't just take our word for it. In a recent study,[11] 20 percussion, wind and string players were given creativity tasks to perform while their brains were scanned. They were asked to come up with creative uses for household objects and, compared to a control group of non-musicians, on average came up with 14 more. Scans of their brain showed that, when working on the creative

[11]'Enhanced Divergent Thinking and Creativity in Musicians: A behavioral and near-infrared spectroscopy study', C. Gibson, B.S. Folley and S. Park, *Brain and Cognition*, 2008.

tasks, the musicians showed more symmetrical blood flow between their brain hemispheres than the non-musicians did. They used both halves of their noggins pretty well.

When musicians create *original* music they use different parts of their brains compared to when performing music they already know.

For example,[12] research has shown that jazz musicians, when improvising jazz, use different parts of their brains as opposed to when playing jazz from memory. These performances didn't take place in a cool jazz dive; however, the highly-trained musicians were on their backs, knees bent up, heads inside fMRI brain scanners and playing the keyboards only with their right hands. Now there's a novel act. Results showed that during improvisation the large portion of the brain responsible for monitoring one's own performance (the *dorsolateral prefrontal cortex*) completely shuts down. 'The researchers explain that, just as over-thinking a jump shot can cause a basketball player to fall out of the zone and perform poorly, the suppression of inhibitory, self-monitoring brain mechanisms helps to promote the free flow of novel ideas and impulses.'[13] The brain pattern is similar to that seen in people when they are dreaming.

Yet you don't have to be an accomplished musician to experience the positive effect music can have on creative performance. Just listening to certain types of music enhances creativity. Try Joan Ambrosio Dalza's *Piva*, for instance, the fourth movement of George Frederic Handel's *Music for the Royal Fireworks*, or the final movement of Joseph Haydn's *The Creation*. At one ad agency we know, when driving to big presentations at their client's offices the agency team would crank up Richard Wagner's *Flight of the*

[12]'Neural Substrates of Spontaneous Musical Performance: An fMRI Study of Jazz Improvisation', Charles J. Limb and Allen A. Braun in *PLoS ONE*, 27 February 2008. It was funded by the National Institute on Deafness and Other Communication Disorders (NIDCD).

[13]'Large Portion of Brain Switches Off and Lets Creativity Flow in Jazz Improvisations', from **www.terradaily.com**, 27 February 2008.

Valkyries to get themselves ready.[14] Music is processed in both sides of the brain and it is thought to coordinate right-brain imagery with left-brain analysis so as to help solve problems more creatively (try Erich Wolfgang Korngold's *Violin Concerto*, first movement).[15]

Music is one of the few things in the world that breaks through language barriers, and being a musician you learn how to connect with somebody emotionally by choosing particular chords or a particular melody. You can use music in business meetings or take a ten-minute break to listen to a piece of music and it will actually tune everybody together. Before that everyone might have been thinking about a million things – 'I need to put on the washing' or 'I forgot to phone my dog' – but you put on a piece of classical music, ABBA, or whatever music you like, and suddenly everybody's on the same plane. It puts everyone on the same wavelength momentarily. When played a piece of classical music, anthropologists have found that African villagers, who have never heard anything like it before, all describe similar emotions when they hear it. In a powerful scene in the film *The Shawshank Redemption*, wrongly convicted prisoner Andy (played by Tim Robbins) finds a recording of Mozart's *Marriage of Figaro*. Knowing how much trouble he'll get into, but doing it anyway, he barricades himself in the warden's office and plays this beautiful music, an aria called *Che Soave Zeffiretto*, or *What a Gentle Breeze*, over the

[14]This is the same music that Lt Colonel Gilgore, the air cavalry commander played by Robert Duvall in the film *Apocalypse Now*, blasts out from his helicopter as he lays waste to a North Vietnamese village. 'I love the smell of Napalm in the morning,' he famously says in another scene.

[15]In 1993 a group of researchers at the University of Wisconsin discovered that when college students listened to ten minutes of a sonata by Mozart, their performance in an IQ test rose by 8–10 points. What became known as the 'Mozart Effect' spawned a whole industry of music CDs and DVDs for parents to play to their toddlers and even unborn infants to boost their IQs. The test done on the college students was actually a spatial task, one that required them to manipulate objects in their minds, not specifically an IQ test, which suggests that while intelligence might not actually be enhanced by listening to music, spatial reasoning, a key part of creativity, might.

prison PA system. It transfixes every hardened inmate and prison guard. They stand frozen, staring up at the speakers as they are momentarily transported to another, better place.[16] Check out our website for music to download (**www.businessplayground.com**).

Dr Adam Anderson of the University of Toronto wanted to see how listening to music impacts people's mood and creative ability.[17] To create a positive or negative mood people listened to happy or sad music and were asked to think about happy or sad things. When in a happy mood they did well on the creative tasks, but not so well on other tasks. 'If you are doing something that requires you to be creative or in a think tank, you want to be in a place with good mood,' says Dr Anderson.[18] 'For example if you are having difficulty solving a problem, a typical reaction is to get angry. But that can actually make it harder to solve the problem. One prescription is to go out and play and get yourself in a good mood, then come back to the problem.' It's thought that a part of the brain called the *amygdala* might be responsible. **The amygdala triggers fear and that shuts down the part of the brain that makes us creative, but when we're happy the amygdala is oh so quiet**[19]**... shhhh.**

[16]No, not Starbucks.

[17]'Happy Mood Improves Creative Thinking but May Lead to Distraction', Adam Anderson, *Proceedings of the National Academy of Sciences*, December 2006.

[18]'Happy Emotions Boost Creativity', *ABC News*, 19 December 2006.

[19]We love Björk.

But, being in a good mood actually has a negative impact on some other types of mental tasks. Says the good doctor, 'If you are doing some form of task that requires focus and many details of calculation, strangely, it might be better to be in a negative mood because the negative mood can filter out everything else.' Negative moods help people focus. 'Under a negative mood,' he says, 'we see the world through a porthole. But under a positive mood, we see the world through a big window.' Another study found that physicians in a positive mood solve problems more creatively than those in a neutral mood.[20] Positive emotions inhibit logical reasoning and make it difficult to detect strong versus weak arguments. So, depending on the problem you want solving, choose your accountant and physician very carefully.

And, don't tell the kids, but playing certain video games can produce emotions that give a creative boost. As part of her graduate thesis, Elizabeth Hutton and a professor S. Shyam Sundar of Penn State University got 98 students to play the videogame *Dance Dance Revolution* to see if it would affect players' problem-solving abilities. If you've never watched this game being played, it's quite a spectacle – players stand on a platform with flashing arrows arranged in a cross shape, and dance to the music by moving their feet quickly on to each arrow as it lights up. The researchers found[21] that players with a high degree of arousal and positive mood were more likely to have new ideas for problem solving. But creativity scores were the highest for players with low arousal and negative mood. Happy *or* sad people are creative, while angry or relaxed people are not. 'The key is to generate emotion,' they concluded.

[20]'Positive Affect Influences Creative Problem Solving and Reported Source of Practice Satisfaction in Physicians', C. Estrada, A.M. Isen and M.J. Young, *Organizational Behavior and Human Decision Processes*, 1994.

[21]'Video Games Can Make Us Creative If Spark Is Right', *Science Daily*, 5 May 2008.

Doing some form of aerobic exercise can also make us more creative. A 2005 study[22] looked at how doing aerobic exercise would affect people's creative performance compared to not doing any. And, guess what, the couch potatoes lost. Some people were randomly picked to do the creative tasks immediately following 30 minutes of running, fast walking, swimming, cycling on a stationary bike or stair climbing. Another group was politely asked to do exercise for 30 minutes and then given a two-hour break with their feet up before doing the tasks, while a third group did the creative task after having done no exercise that day, the slobs. The results showed that, 'Instances of aerobic exercise significantly impacted the creative processes of the participants, and these effects were shown to endure over a two-hour period.' Why this happens is likely to be to do with blood flowing through the brain: the increased blood flow delivering nutrients in the form of glucose, and perhaps the endorphins released by the increased oxygen in the bloodstream making new neural connections in the brain.

Music, video games and aerobic exercise all affect mood and in turn creative performance. In most office environments doing any of these activities might be frowned upon – having a colleague do aerobics while you're on a conference call might be a little off-putting – but the point is, when we're in creative mode we often need to do something else other than stare at the computer screen waiting for inspiration. **We need to give our brain a rest, or lift our mood, or get the blood flowing, and so taking a break for a while is well worth it. And now you've got the scientific evidence to prove that, while it might not look like you're working hard, you really are!**

[22]'Aerobic Exercise and Cognitive Creativity: Immediate and Residual Effects', D.M. Blanchette, S.P. Ramocki, J.N. O'del and M.S. Casey, *Creativity Research Journal*, 2005.

THERE'S A HOLE IN MY HEAD

On the subject of how increasing the blood flow to the brain through exercise or video gaming increases creativity, some people believe that drilling a hole in their head will increase blood flow and so have the same effect. We're not recommending this, by the way, just mentioning it in passing. This is called *trepanation* and involves making a small hole in the skull to decrease the pressure on the brain to increase the volume of blood flowing through it. **Trepanning is an ancient surgical practice and a trepanned skull was recently found in France that is believed to be 7,000 years old.** Not surprisingly, though, there aren't many people nowadays that practise it, one reason maybe being that if you practise it and don't do such a great job you'll probably wind up dead.

One person who has tried and lived to tell the tale is Peter Halvorson. In a 1998 interview[23] he described how, 26 years previously in a small room in Holland, he used an injection of anaesthetic, a scalpel, four drill bits and an electric power drill controlled by his foot to make the hole. 'I could hear a gurgling, and I could feel the shifting of volume in the brain water,' says Halvorson when describing the moment he broke through the skull. 'There was a warm feeling as my metabolism cranked up a bit.' He did the trepanation for enlightenment – we might suggest a good book instead, but, oh well – and according to Pete the result of the procedure was more energy, more drive and more focus, and it returned him to the 'buoyancy' he had as a child.

[23]'You Need It … Like a Hole in the Head. If You're Looking for Enlightenment, Here's the Drill', Michael Colton, *Washington Post*, 31 May 1998.

The man responsible for a modern-day resurgence of popular interest (we admit *resurgence* may be overstating it somewhat) in trepanation is a Dutch librarian called Bart Hughes, who in the 1960s had trepanned himself and lived to tell the tale in his book, *Trepanation: The Cure for Psychosis*. **According to Hughes, gravity and age rob adults of the creativity and energy that a child possesses.** While a baby's skull has a *fontanel* – the soft spot – that allows the brain to pulsate, by adulthood the skull has hardened and so the brain can no longer pulsate as it did and that, together with good old gravity, saps more blood from the head. Trepanation, Hughes believes, reverses this loss of blood volume and gives you the feeling you get from standing on your head for a few minutes, or from sustained aerobic activity. You know, a bit of a head rush.

Another recent trepanner was Oxford University professor Lord James Neidpath, who taught Bill Clinton when the ex-US President was a Rhodes scholar at Oxford. The prof. had decided to do it because his wife had already tried it and spoke very highly of the results. And, according to Paul McCartney in a 1986 interview with the magazine *Q*, John Lennon was also interested in the idea. John asked Paul and wife Linda if, 'You fancy getting the trepanning done?'[24] They never did. You can learn more at **www.trepan.com**, the website for the International Trepanation Advocacy Group (ITAG). Drills are available at most good DIY shops, bandages at your high-street chemist ...

[24] 'An Innocent Man?', Chris Salewicz, *Q*, October 1986.

MOVE ONE SPACE FORWARD TO THE NEXT CHAPTER ... OR ROLL THE DICE

So, creativity involves thinking more broadly than the more sensible, analytical parts of our brains allow us to do. Making time for distractions that keep our minds off the problems we are trying to solve creatively can make the solutions better than they would otherwise have been, and in business that means going off to do something else for a while. All people tend to switch between different methods of problem solving: the ones that use analysis and the other insight that leads to an 'A-ha!' moment – they sometimes subconsciously decide which method to use even before they know what problem they are going to solve – but some people use insight more than others. **It's likely that some people are in fact more creative than other people, but we all have the ability to think creatively and certain activities can bring out that ability.** Musicians, for instance, tend to think creatively, but just listening to music also has a positive effect on creativity, as does playing video games or aerobic activity, by putting us in a positive mood or increasing blood flow to the brain. The downside of being in a positive mood is that it can make us less effective at making logical decisions. In the next few chapters we introduce fun techniques for coming up with ideas, all of which tap into the side of our brains that does the diverse thinking. You'll be pleased to know that hardly any of them involve the need for sharp instruments.

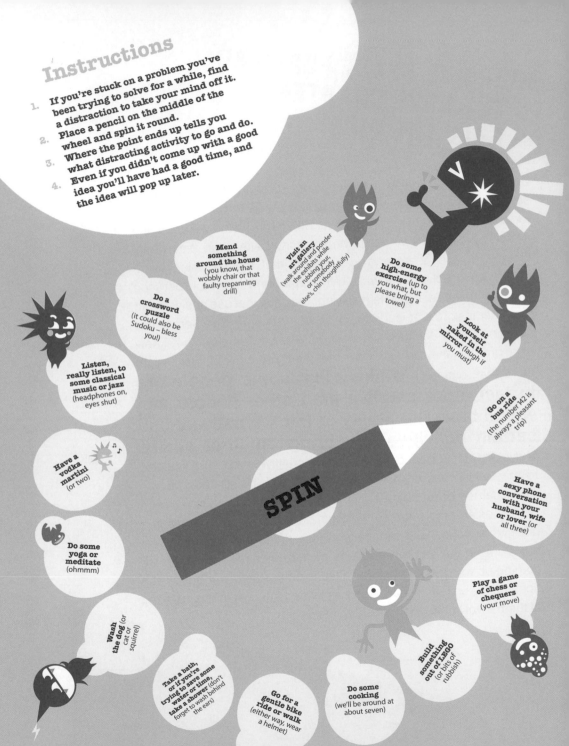

Instructions

1. If you're stuck on a problem you've been trying to solve for a while, find a distraction to take your mind off it.
2. Place a pencil on the middle of the wheel and spin it round.
3. Where the point ends up tells you what distracting activity to go and do.
4. Even if you didn't come up with a good idea you'll have had a good time, and the idea will pop up later.

Mend something around the house (you know, that wobbly chair or that faulty trepanning drill)

Visit an art gallery (walk around and ponder the exhibits while rubbing your, or somebody else's, chin thoughtfully)

Do some high-energy exercise (up to you what, but please bring a towel)

Do a crossword puzzle (it could also be Sudoku – bless you!)

Look at yourself naked in the mirror (laugh if you must)

Listen, really listen, to some classical music or jazz (headphones on, eyes shut)

Go on a bus ride (the number 142 is always a pleasant trip)

Have a vodka martini (or two)

Have a sexy phone conversation with your husband, wife or lover (or all three)

SPIN

Do some yoga or meditate (ohmmm)

Play a game of chess or chequers (your move)

Wash the dog (or cat or squirrel)

Build something out of LEGO (or bits of rubbish)

Take a bath, or if you're trying to save some water or time, take a shower (don't forget to wash behind the ears)

Go for a gentle bike ride or walk (either way, wear a helmet)

Do some cooking (we'll be around at about seven)

BOARD GAME: WHEEL OF DISTRACTION

How it works: When we have a clear creative challenge, and after spending some time thinking through a problem, the brain often needs a rest from concentrated thought so it can wander and make less obvious connections. But more than just giving it a rest, if we task the brain with something distracting we actually help it solve the creative challenge we set out by allowing it to do its work unencumbered by stumbling blocks like logic and analysis.

How to play: Players spend some time framing the creative problem they're trying to solve and then they do something absorbing and totally unrelated to the problem by randomly picking a distraction from the wheel. Choose one by spinning a pencil on the centre of the wheel and seeing where the pointy bit ends up.

Light – Birthday – Stick   *(answer: Candle)*

Cross – Rain – Tie   *(answer: Bow)*

Boot – Summer – Ground   *(answer: Camp)*

Manners – Round – Tennis   *(answer: Table)*

Health – Taker – Less   *(answer: Care)*

Off – Trumpet – Atomic   *(answer: Blast)*

Carpet – Alert – Ink   *(answer: Red)*

Test – Runner – Map   *(answer: Road)*

Man – Glue – Star   *(answer: Super)*

Stick – Maker – Point   *(answer: Match)*

Foot – Collection – Out   *(answer: Stamp)*

Line – Fruit – Drunk   *(answer: Punch)*

Mate – Shoes – Total   *(answer: Running)*

Land – Hand – House   *(answer: Farm)*

Bump – Throat – Sum   *(answer: Lump)*

CHAPTER SIX
BRAIN FLASH

Using visualisation to come up with creative solutions.

Picture this, a boat on a river.

If a picture is worth a thousand words and the pen is mightier than the sword, then surely a crayon must be a weapon of mass destruction? Or something like that. **The same is true of music, you can never adequately express the ideas in music through words – you have to hear it.** Ken Robinson in his book, *Out of Our Minds: Learning to be Creative*, gives this example: 'The composer Gustav Mahler was sitting in his studio completing a new piano piece. As he was playing, one of his students came into his room and listened quietly. At the end of the piece the student said, "Maestro, that was wonderful. What is it about?" Mahler turned to him and said, "It's about this." And he played it again.'

THE PETRI DISH FOR IDEAS

In 1966 researchers at San Francisco State College published the results of a pilot study into how psychedelic drugs might impact creativity. They tested the effects of LSD-25 and mescaline on 27 professionally employed males[1] (honestly, they really did). Tentative findings led them to conclude that, 'Psychedelic agents seem to facilitate creative problem-solving, particularly in the "illumination phase". The results also suggest that various degrees of increased creative ability may continue for at least some weeks subsequent to a psychedelic problem-solving session.' Based upon what the subjects in the study said about their experiences with the drugs,

[1]'Psychedelic Agents in Creative Problem-Solving: a Pilot Study', Willis W. Harman, Robert H. McKim, Robert E. Mogar, James Fadiman and Myron J. Stolaroff, *Psychological Reports*, 1966, 19, pp. 211–227, Southern Universities Press 1966, Monograph Supplement 2-V19.

I often use different methods to 'break the plane' with artists I'm working with who are experiencing some sort of block in their creative flow.

Bob Dylan was going through a period in the early 1990s when he was a little lost and searching for inspiration. Instead of us trying to make a record, or finish words to songs (we had recorded about 20 sketches), we went out and shot a film instead. It was much more fun, with just me filming on 8mm cine cameras and Bob wearing a 1920s top hat on his head wandering around Camden Town like the Pied Piper (we ended up being followed by a bunch of people who could not believe what they were seeing, so we got them to act in it too). This was in London in broad daylight and we had no-one with us as security, or any assistants, just the two of us and my three-year old son, Django. We were laughing and having great fun making up sequences and then shooting them on the spot. You can see where some of this footage ended up if you go on YouTube and type in 'Bob Dylan Blood in my Eyes,' as later I asked Sophie Muller to edit some of it together for a video to that song and she did a great job.

There is no point in sitting staring at the wall trying to be inspired when the whole world is outside waiting to play with you, or for you to play with it. For instance, another time I took Bob Dylan on my houseboat with my mother, Sadie, and a few other people just to 'break the plane' and we went down the canals with acoustic guitars and a tape recorder making up stuff while my mum cooked soup. When we got off the boat I took him to Speakers' Corner in Hyde Park where people get on a soapbox and say what they want. Bob stood for a long time listening with his hood over his head and heckling a few times. We had a great day and he later wrote a song about it, called *TV Talkin' Song*.

the researchers believe that certain aspects of the psychedelic experience support creativity, key among them being a heightened ability for visual imagery and fantasy. Other studies since have also looked at the relationship between drugs like LSD and creativity.[2]

Language processing occurs in the sensible, analytical left half of the brain, whereas visualising is done in its more creative right-sided counterpart, so it stands to reason that creativity benefits from the use of our visual skills, and when we want to put the ideas into words we can get a little help from little old leftie. **To Leonardo da Vinci the ability to think was inseparable from the ability to visualise, the eye was an instrument of thought.**

Here's a simple and legal technique for using your visual powers to think through a problem. Find a comfortable chair in quiet space, kick off your shoes, remove your hat and loosen your tie. Take a large pad of paper and a bunch of pens and pencils and sit down. That's it, now just relax. Clear your mind of the stuff you need to do (… did you tell Bob the meeting was cancelled? Don't worry about it, he'll be fine. And that big presentation you need to write, the one for the board? Just forget about it, not doing it will save some paper …) and start to think about the creative problem you need to solve. On the left half of the page start to sketch out a picture of what things are like now, not a detailed diagram, just the basic elements that convey your thoughts about the situation. You can add in some simple labels to make it clearer if you want, but this is for you not for anyone else so if they don't get it, that's their problem, they shouldn't be looking anyway.

[2]We liked 'A Psychobiographical Analysis of Brian Douglas Wilson: Creativity, drugs, and models of schizophrenic and affective disorders', Stefano Belli, *Personality and Individual Differences*, Vol. 46, Issue 8, June 2009, pp. 809–819.

Now on the right-hand half of the page, sketch out how you want things to be. What is your vision for success? Where do you want this to end up? There need to be some big differences between what you drew on the left and what you're going to draw on the right side of the page and you can even exaggerate to make the point. If *solving the traffic congestion in LA* were the problem, for instance, to highlight the differences between what the traffic situation is now and what we'd like it be, we might draw the exact opposite of what is the current picture of jams and snarl-ups. Perhaps we would sketch a vision in which there are absolutely no cars on the roads, or there are no roads at all, just green fields, parks and trees. Ah … that feels nice.

Don't scrimp on the picture. **Take time with the details so it is as vivid as it can be.** Make it so you can actually picture yourself in that boat on the river, and so you can almost taste the orangey-ness of the nearby tangerine trees and marmalade skies. Now, having sketched out the before and after, the current situation and your vision for success, ask yourself (out loud if you want): 'What are the barriers between how things are and how I want them to be?' Perhaps you see one barrier as the design of your product, or maybe not enough people know how amazing your services are, or a lack of communication between departments means initiatives don't get followed through properly? Whatever the barriers are, find ways to represent them through your sketches and add them into the drawing in a different coloured pen (yeah, that purple is a good shade, try that one). Again, it's a good idea to label what you've drawn. And finally, in another colour (not that turquoise, it'll clash horribly with the lime green you used earlier), sketch ideas for ways to break down the barriers.

But first, take a breather. The right side of your brain needs time to come up with ideas sparked by what you have in your sketch. Stand up. Stretch. Sponge the marker-pen stain off your shirt. Touch your toes. Lick your nose. Lick someone else's nose. Give yourself a while to absorb all the information you've laid out on your big piece of paper. You see before you, in glorious Technicolor, the problem, the vision, and the barriers to getting there and you'll find that as you stare at it you'll start to come up with ways to draw potential solutions to break down the barriers, ones that if you'd just tried to write it all down you'd never have seen. **By not relying on words you have freed up the visual power of your brain.**

Now show it to your boss or partner or neighbour. Don't say anything, just hand it over with a smug 'Aren't I the clever one?' smile on your face and walk out humming to yourself. Actually, on second thoughts, don't do that, you might not exactly get the reaction you'd hoped for. The sketch is for you and you alone. Later, if there's some good stuff in there you might want to adapt the sketch into a simple diagram – that's always a good way to explain something – but for now use it as a way to capture some ideas. Pin the sketch somewhere you can see it so each time you go past you can add something or make a note on it and it can become a Petri dish for new ideas.

COLLAGING

As we said a couple of chapters back, many challenges are best tackled creatively by first pulling them apart and tinkering around with each piece (whether as cherries or fish bones) before putting them back together again. A technique sometimes called *collaging* involves conducting a brainstorm with a mix of folks of all shapes

A method I have found very useful for creating something from nothing is this. I start by taking a photograph, usually of a very interesting woman, if any are available. But if not then it can be of anything – an empty room, a book cabinet – it doesn't really matter. What matters is that you have frozen a moment in time. Now, I look at that picture and give it a title. For instance, last week I took a photo on the staircase of an actress called Natalie Mendoza. We stared at the picture for a while, giving it possible titles like for a movie poster. I came up with 'If Looks Could Kill' and then we talked about what that could mean. Such as, someone could be so beautiful that it ruined their life, or it could mean literally that someone has so much pent-up anger that they can't hide the hate.

So that started a song:

If Looks Could Kill then you've got the skill
And I must have died a thousand times

Then a short film script. It could be about a woman (played by Natalie) who had been so frozen that she actually forgot who she was. One day she wakes up and doesn't recognise a thing, only that she has been tied and bound inside her own mind, which we see in the film. She spends days struggling to break free, and when she escapes and opens a door it's into the blinding sunlight. And as she steps outside we realise it's from a Hollywood movie-set trailer where she is met by her assistant, make-up lady and the Assistant Director. They walk her to the set, which is all totally unreal to her, but slowly through the movie and the tiny bubble of the movie-making world she realises who she really is! Crazy all back to front … in other words 'reality is an illusion' that occurs due to a lack of scripts!

And now from the same photo shoot we have a song, a film treatment and from another photo I took that day of Natalie we came up with the name 'Butterfly'. Having been inspired by this creative exercise, several months later Natalie came back to Los Angeles with a concept, which I renamed 'Butterfli', and is now being produced into a graphic novel, an anime mobile series and a feature film starring Natalie.[3]

Another project I've been working on started life as a little game inside a Nokia mobile phone, this time for a very talented singer I found called Cindy Gomez, who I first met when I was on *Larry King Live* with Ringo Starr, and she had just arrived to perform as a back-up singer. This is the very first time an artist has debuted inside a mobile phone game. And one of the songs in that game is called *Street Dancing.* So then I started working on an idea for a film called *Street Dancing*, about a boy in India who finds and plays with the game on the phone and he starts really wanting to be a dancer, and enters a competition called – guess what? – 'Street Dancing'. I then thought this could also be a TV format. All things line up, like the stars, and you realise that from this song idea inside a mobile dancing game, it can be a feature film, in a TV show, or even as a lifestyle brand. And, lo and behold, this is what's happening.

Now you are thinking: 'God, what kind of job does Dave have just taking pictures of talented women and dreaming up ideas about how to have more fun with a song or a film or a gadget?' Well, you are absolutely right! It's what I choose to do, but the amount of work that then goes into executing the song, or 3-D game, or whatever it is we are doing, makes the difference between larking about and running a creative company.

If I was running a company that made tennis balls and had a marketing meeting I might still use this method of taking a picture of a woman then staring at it and saying to myself, 'Now how does that picture relate to balls?' No, seriously. I would give it a title relating to my business like '40–love' or 'Game, set and match', put a web address on the photo, then when people went there it would be a humorous spoof dating site all based around tennis in which the same girl in the photo invites you to join the club. Once inside there'd be a virtual world and you can chat to our girl, but just when things get steamy the screen fills up with tennis balls and you have to give your email to become a member. I'm not saying this is a good idea, I'm just saying how the idea can come about through visualisation.

---

[3]Natalie has been cast as the female lead in U2's Broadway musical *Spiderman*, directed by Julie Taymor.

and sizes to sketch out the different parts of a problem, and then putting the individual sketches together as a collage. The group can then use the collage as a way to spark new ideas.

Here's how. **Split up the problem into as many components as there are people in the brainstorm group** (somewhere between four and eight is usually a good number, but it depends on how many comfortable chairs you have available) and get them each to start doing a detailed sketch as a way to solve their bit of the problem. Take traffic congestion in LA as an example. Say there are seven people in the group, we could pretty easily split the problem into seven different smaller problems. Let's call them our seven *problemettes*:

1 **Too many cars.**

2 **People driving alone.**

3 **No good alternative transport.**

4 **The need to travel to get to work.**

5 **People in LA love cars.**

6 **Too few major roads.**

7 **Accidents on roads causing delays.**

The choice of seven was purely random. It could have been four, five, six, eight, or whatever number, and so long as we've got the main components of the problem down we're OK, you'll find that you will cut according to your cloth. To expand on the analogy (see the section on metaphors coming up), if you haven't got much cloth available you will end up with a smaller suit, perhaps with shorts rather than trousers and sleeves that only come down to your elbows. If you've got yards of the stuff, you could make a suit where you can wear stilts and the trouser legs still reach the ground. We know that doesn't make sense, but we liked the metaphor anyway, the point being so long as you have a handful of people in the brainstorm there are ways to split up the problem so each of them has a piece of it to tackle.

Here is what's known as a mind map. It's from a series done for Coco de Mer, the 'Erotic Emporiums' I am a partner in, together with Anita and Gordon Roddick's two daughters, Sam and Justine. Anita, Gordon, Sam, Justine and I took part in a mind map session hosted by John Kao, the innovation expert and business strategist who wrote the brilliant Harvard Business book *Jamming*, and mind-map artist Lesley Evans, working on five-foot pieces of paper.[4] This is just one of about ten mind maps that came out of that session.

[4]*Jamming: The Art and Discipline of Business Creativity*, John Kao, HarperCollins 1996.

Now as an example of how this works, at random let's take one of the traffic problemettes. We're going to take number two, and as a solution to the bit about people driving alone we make a sketch of lots of people sharing the same car (they'd probably be laughing, slapping one another on the back, making rabbit ears and sharing snacks, but who knows for sure). When each of the brainstormers has done their sketch for their assigned problemette they can show it to the rest of group. The others should throw in their comments (no heckling, please) and their ideas for how to improve what's been drawn, making sure it's done in the spirit of positive collaboration. Then once the sketches are combined into a collage the resulting picture will hopefully represent some great thinking by the group, delivered in a fresh visual way, and it might even trigger some wonderful new ideas.

IT'S LIKE A ...
WELL, IT'S LIKE A SIMILE

The researchers at San Francisco State College, who decades ago experimented with psychedelic agents like LSD and mescaline and their effects on creativity, found one reason subjects in the study gave for their improvement was their enhanced ability to play spontaneously with hypotheses, metaphors, paradox, transformations and relationships. Making comparisons between concepts can help highlight their similarities and differences and spark ideas that might be of help. **For instance, a camera is like an eye and an umbrella like a canopy of leaves. The stronger the visual imagery involved in the simile, the richer the comparisons will be.** What is your business challenge similar to? Does it remind you of something in nature or from another field?

NASA was trying to design a satellite tethered to a space station by a 60-mile-long length of wire[5] but found that when they tried to reel it in it started swinging out in ever-increasing arcs, which took way too long and put a lot of stress on the wire. By seeing that the satellite tethered to a space station was similar to a person holding a yo-yo on a string, and understanding how the winding power created by the spin of the yo-yo pulls it back in, they were able to come up with a better solution for reeling back the satellite. Instead of the space station winding in the satellite, a small motor on the satellite would pull itself into the space station, so cutting out the wild swinging movements (we're convinced NASA are now practising other yo-yo tricks, such as walking the dog, with their satellites).

Or, take the invention of the tasty curvy crisps, Pringles. These wavy wonders were developed as a result of a quest to find a way to package crisps in a more efficient way. When packed loosely in bags, regular crisps take up a lot of room, but when packed in smaller bags they break up and crumble. **Thinking about the similarities between crisps and leaves helped the smarty-pants at manufacturer Procter and Gamble to find a solution.** The researchers thought about how dry leaves break apart easily, while moist ones do not. If leaves are pressed together when moist and then allowed to dry out, there are no gaps between them and so can be packed tightly together without breaking. Bingo. So that's what they tried. Organic chemist Fredrick J. Bauer developed a foil-lined tube with a resealable plastic lid that allowed the Pringles to be packed in tightly together so they wouldn't break when moved around. Incidentally, the cremated remains of Mr Bauer, who died in 2008, are buried in a Pringles container.[6] Not on sale in any shop near you.

[5] 'Improving the Creativity of Organisational Work Groups', Leigh Thompson, *Academy of Management Executive*, 2003, Vol. 17, No. 1.

[6] It's true. It was reported in the *Guardian* newspaper on 2 June 2008.

Think of traffic congestion in LA being like a patient with clogged arteries.[7] Now we have a new way of looking at the problem, one we can visualise, we can start to imagine cures for people with heart disease, such as surgery and a healthier diet. Surgery could suggest putting in a new road to bypass blockages; having a healthier diet suggests preventing the roads being clogged in the first place by reducing the number of accidents or the number of cars on the roads. **Alternatively, why not look at things that are dissimilar between a situation and the creative problem we're trying to solve? For instance: traffic congestion in LA is really *unlike* a mountain stream.** It is neither clean, nor fast, nor peaceful. And to make it more similar to a stream we would use cleaner cars, keep the flow of traffic moving and introduce noise dampening around the roads (also mountain streams flow in just one direction, so consider one-way roads as a solution). Using an evocative visual simile like this we can picture what this new situation would look like. Imagine sitting next to a mountain stream and think how it makes you feel. Maybe draw a picture of the scene or find one on the web and then start to think about how to recreate that same feeling of peace and calm for the problem you're trying to solve.

[7] It reminds of us of a Monty Python sketch in which courtesans use similes to fling insults. James McNeil Whistler (John Cleese) tells the Prince of Wales (Terry Jones) 'Your majesty is like a stream of bat's piss,' and when the Prince looks insulted, he claims it was George Bernard Shaw (Michael Palin) who had said it originally. Shaw denies it and then tries to explain the insult by saying what he meant by it was that 'You shine out like a shaft of gold when all around is dark,' which the Prince finds most charming.

METAPHORICALLY SPEAKING

In the last film that Peter Sellers made, *Being There*, Sellers plays Chance, a simple-minded gardener who has spent his whole life tending the garden of 'The Old Man'. Chance has had no education, and apart from what he's learned from television he has no experience of the outside world. When The Old Man dies, Chance is told to leave the house and, while wandering the streets carrying all his possessions in a single suitcase, is knocked over on the street by a car owned by a Mrs Benjamin Rand. Mrs Rand, wanting no trouble for her powerful husband, an advisor to the President of the United States, takes him to her estate to be tended to by her private doctor. Neither she nor her husband realise that 'Chauncey Gardiner' (the name they thought they heard when he introduced himself as 'Chance, the gardener') is just a simpleton and instead thinks that he has great wisdom, a wisdom that he delivers through metaphors. In this extract from the novel by Jerzy Kosinski,[8] who also wrote the screenplay[9] for the film, Chance is brought into a conversation between Mr Rand and the President.

[8]*Being There*, Jerzy Kosinski, Grove/Atlantic, 1970.

[9]His screenplay for *Being There* was nominated for a Golden Globe in 1980 and won the BAFTA in 1981.

The men began a long conversation. Chance understood almost nothing of what they were saying, even though they often looked in his direction, as if to invite his participation. Chance thought they purposefully spoke in another language for reasons of secrecy, when suddenly the President addressed him: 'And you, Mr Gardiner? What do you think about the bad season on The Street?'

Chance shrank. He felt that the roots of his thoughts had been suddenly yanked out of their wet earth and thrust, tangled, into the unfriendly air. He stared at the carpet. Finally he spoke: 'In a garden,' he said, 'growth has its season. There are spring and summer, but there is also fall and winter. And then spring and summer again. As long as the roots are not severed, all is well and all will be well.' He raised his eyes. Rand was looking at him, nodding. The President seemed quite pleased.

'I must admit, Mr Gardiner,' the President said, 'that what you've just said is one of the most refreshing and optimistic statements I've heard in a very, very long time.' He rose and stood erect, with his back to the fireplace. 'Many of us forget that nature and society are one! Yes, though we have tried to cut ourselves off from nature, we are still part of it. Like nature, our economic system remains, in the long run, stable and rational, and that's why we must not fear to be at its mercy.' The President hesitated for a moment, then turned to Rand. 'We welcome the inevitable seasons of nature, yet we are upset by the seasons of the economy! How foolish of us!' He smiled at Chance. 'I envy Mr Gardiner his good solid sense. This is just what we lack on Capitol Hill.'

Any re-working of language (what I call 'Pasta Talk' because it's the stuff idea spaghetti is made of) is good for the brain, as you have to think in parallel. A good exercise is telling a story in mechanic speak – like, 'I was trying to wrench myself out of the situation before I blew a gasket,' signed 'Full Throttle'.

This is not a business solution, but when you get good at it you can apply that way of thinking to solve a business problem. In other words simplify it, a bit like Chauncy Gardiner did. Jazz players have a language, a kind of slang. All musicians have it. Weird things like, 'Don't drag the donkey'. Actually, I just made that up, but it's a good way of describing a situation where you've bought or hired a pony to carry your workload and now you seem to be carrying his.

Metaphors conjure up images that can spark ideas. Start by writing up the problem as a simple question, for instance: 'How can people in LA spend less time in their cars?' We might choose baking as a metaphor and rewrite the problem as 'How can bakers spend less time making bread?' and then picture the baker and his bread-making endeavours and imagine how he might spend less time doing them. For instance, the baker might consider:

Making bigger batches of bread.

Selling less bread.

Making bigger loaves.

Outsourcing the baking to someone else.

Bringing in some assistants.

Closing the bakery altogether.

The ideas for the baking question are metaphors for our traffic problem. Making bigger batches of bread could mean encouraging people to travel in bigger groups, such as in buses or car pools, to reduce the congestion. Or closing the bakery might make us think about closing some roads to force people to travel less. Perhaps they can earn their bread without going to the office so much.

MOVE ONE SPACE FORWARD TO THE NEXT CHAPTER ... OR ROLL THE DICE

Sometimes words are just not enough. Language processing occurs largely in the sensible analytical left half of the brain, whereas visualisation takes place mainly in the more creative right half. **Making pictures, whether actual sketches or verbal ones such as similes and metaphors, can free up our minds to think more creatively.** In fact, when people aren't allowed to sketch and have to rely on words to process information they tend find it difficult to restructure it and discover new way of looking at it. Techniques for visualising problems and finding creative solutions include sketching it out on your own, taking photos, or doing a group collaging exercise that tasks people with creating a sketch together. Similes and metaphors help spark the imagination by allowing us to picture how a problem we're working on is similar or dissimilar to something that might at first seem totally unrelated. In the next chapter we look at how to creatively collaborate with others to build ideas. Gather round, everybody.

Instructions

1. Decide on a problem to solve.
2. Take turns throwing a pair of dice to pick a square on the board, the first die giving the number along the bottom, the second up the side.
3. Each player comes up with an idea sparked by the visual in the square.
4. The best idea gets a point.
5. The winner is the player with the most points after five rounds (or however many rounds players have decided to play).

BOARD GAME: BRAIN FLASH

How it works: Visual stimuli help in the generation of new ideas by tapping directly into the right side of the brain, where creative processing takes place, without being inhibited by the left side, the one that uses language to process thought. So if we take a problem and ask the brain to find connections between it and a visual stimulus, we will potentially end up with some great insights and ideas that we might not have otherwise discovered.

How to play: Players decide on a problem they want to solve and then throw the dice to tell them which visual stimulus on the board they should use to spark ideas to help solve it. For example, if the problem players choose is: how do we improve customer service? and a player throws a 5 and a 3, the square five along and three up shows a picture of some juggling skittles,

and so players might decide to describe the problem as a simile using acrobats – for instance, 'customer service is like juggling skittles because it means being quick and agile.' Then players come up with ideas for ways to ensure staff can help customers very quickly, such as giving them incentives based on speed of response. The image of the juggling skittles could have led to a different simile, one about how 'great customer service is like being an acrobat because it depends on having amazing coordination between departments', in which case players would come up with ideas to improve coordination.

How to win: In each round the player with the best idea gets a point and the winner is the one with the most points after five rounds (or however many rounds the players have agreed to play).

CHAPTER SEVEN
THE IDEA COMMUNE

Working (and playing) with others to come up with ideas.

Communes are happy places where everyone pulls together with a common goal in mind, whether it's growing vegetables or sleeping with one another. (We shouldn't mention that Charles Manson, who with some of his followers in 1969 slaughtered seven people at the home of actress Sharon Tate, ran a commune on a Spahn Ranch. Manson, by the way, was an aspiring songwriter and according to musician Neil Young, who knew Manson, a record company executive had told Neil, 'This guy, you know, he's good. He's just a little out of control.'[1])

The traditional creative process can be, unlike the free and easy spirit of communes, very competitive, with each person trying to hold on to and own his or her idea at the expense of any others. Where's the harmony in that? **Actually, a bit of healthy competition can sometimes help – people like to be recognised by their peers and rewarded for the things they create – but sometimes you just have to chill and get into the communal spirit of sharing and collaborating for the common good**. After all, coming up with ideas can be a lonely occupation. Many creative geniuses are solitary figures driven by a self-belief and passion that leaves them isolated and cut off from the outside world. Many end up not washing for days, eating cat food and withdrawing from society (Dave's wife is always telling him his trousers are on back-to-front or that he has nothing on). We salute them, but move away from them on the bus.

For businesses to be truly creative they need to embrace the spirit of collaboration, not only by tapping into internal resources and those of hired hands, but by working in partnership with other businesses (once thought of as competitors) that share similar goals and have

[1]'Peace, Love and Charlie Manson', Anthony DeCurtis, *The New York Times*, 1 August 2009.

complementary skills. Gone are the days when a silo mentality of total ownership and control was possible or even desirable. Technology has changed all that and the power has shifted into the trigger-happy hands of the masses (the trigger being a computer or mobile phone key, a button on a remote, or whatever other device they might be holding that zaps their attention to something bigger, better, faster). And yet, this same technology has made it possible for businesses who understand the new regime to play, so that the collaborative whole can be greater than the sum of the parts and for ideas to emerge and blossom that no single entity could have created. **What would life be like without Wikipedia, for instance, the online encyclopedia consisting of millions of articles written collaboratively by thousands of volunteers all over the world?**

As we mentioned in Chapter 2, creating an ensemble isn't always easy and it isn't always effective, so you need to use some simple techniques to make it work. Try this as an ice-breaker. Start by setting a clear creative goal (e.g. *we need ideas for a healthy instant snack food*), then gather your brethren around you and ask each one to write down ideas on cards and – here's the sharing bit – put the cards in the middle of the table. They can write as many as they want in the set time (but hey, this is a commune, who needs watches?), then others can pull from the idea pool and add to them and build on them (see the game at the end of the chapter for another fun technique).

It's interesting to get a group of creative people together, often from very different backgrounds, when what they do isn't connected. Mahler's wife used to host these dinners in Vienna to which she'd invite an architect, a composer and a writer and gradually Vienna became a creative capital.[2] So many things come from people with completely different skills and mindsets sitting down at a table together and discussing a problem that's not connected to any of their skills and abilities, and so they're looking at it in a completely different way. I sometimes call that a 'talent brothel'. It's very important for people in business to include outsiders, and not always confine discussions to the insiders who are thinking in the exact same way and are on the exact same railroad track. They need to have some of these diverse people with weird ideas inside the company at every meeting.

I helped create a place in London called 'The Hospital Club' with my friend and Microsoft co-founder, Paul Allen, as a creative members club. We used to joke about it as we are both have slight tendencies to be hypochondriacs, so we would say 'Uh oh, now we have a whole hospital,' which was because when Paul bought the building it was St Paul's Hospital and it was such a derelict mess. It had been abandoned for eight years but it still had the most gross and weird stuff left behind which I will spare you from reading about! It's in the heart of Covent Garden and on seven floors. It has a TV studio, art gallery, recording studio, screening room and restaurant. But, most importantly, it has about five bars and lots of room to sit around and talk one to one or have group conversations. The whole place is run really well and has a calendar of events like Creative Capital, lectures or Writing Salons.

I often wonder why a lot of these giant corporations don't have places like this and why everything has to be so stuffy and uptight – it's so anti-creative an atmosphere. Of course, there are some companies like Pixar or Google, etc., that have realised work and play go good together and they have basketball courts and hang-out places like cool cafes, etc., on site, and I'm sure it helps everyone exchange ideas freely as opposed to everything is a meeting with people sat around an oblong table. Yuck!

[2]Mrs Mahler had all sorts of affairs with the artist community of Vienna over the years. Before marrying Mahler she'd had affairs with artist Gustav Klimt, theatre director Max Burckhard and composer Alexander von Zemlinsky. When married to Gustav she had an affair with architect Walter Gropius, who later became known for his Bauhaus school (they later married), and after Mahler's death, with artist Oskar Kokoschka, then writer Franz Werfel (while still married to second husband Gropius), who she later married. Quite an entertainer that Mrs Mahler.

THE LEADER OF THE PACK

Most people work in businesses in teams in one form or another and, according to the authors of one study on creativity in the workplace, 'Of all of the forces that impinge on people's daily experience of the work environment in these organisations, one of the most immediate and potent is likely to be the leadership of these teams – those "local leaders" who direct and evaluate their work, facilitate or impede their access to resources and information, and in myriad other ways touch their engagement with tasks and with other people.'[3] **To be effective, people running teams of people who are tasked with using creativity to solve problems need certain skills – they need to be good communicators.** They should be able to keep tabs on the progress of projects and use their interpersonal networks to gather information relevant to it. And they should be open to others' ideas and empathetic to the team members' feelings.

OK, so duh. It might seem pretty obvious that how the boss behaves is going to have an impact on our work. But there's more to it than that. Using a questionnaire sent out daily to hundreds of employees across three different industries, the researchers found that *negative behaviours had a more extreme effect than positive ones*. In other words, a bad boss is 'more bad' than a good boss is good, and cutting out destructive behaviours is at least as important as exhibiting positive ones. The dangerous boss behaviours are these: giving out assignments without understanding who has the capabilities needed to do them, or not considering other responsibilities they might have; micromanaging employees' work; and not dealing properly with technical or interpersonal problems. Sound familiar?

[3]'Leader Behaviors and the Work Environment for Creativity: Perceived leader support', Teresa M. Amabile, Elizabeth A. Schatzel, Giovanni B. Moneta and Steven J. Kramer, *The Leadership Quarterly* 15 (2004), pp. 5–32.

The researchers concluded, after their exhaustive study, 'At the broadest level, our study suggests that leaders who wish to support high-level performance must pay careful attention to the details of their own everyday – and seemingly mundane – behavior toward subordinates. What this study has demonstrated, we believe, is the power of ordinary practices.'

It's not just a case of making jokes and giving employees a pat on the back (or a hug around the neck or a kiss upon the lips), good leaders of creative teams need to help individuals move forward with their work and treat them decently as human beings.[4]

According to the conclusions[5] of a two-day colloquium at Harvard Business School with the leaders of companies whose success depends on creativity (we think that's pretty much *every* company, by the way), good leaders don't attempt to manage creativity, they manage *for* creativity, by providing a working environment and culture that allows creativity to flourish. **Leaders should not think of themselves as wellsprings of ideas that employees execute, but as the champions of others' ideas.** In fact, it's a mistake to assume creativity will flow from one source: the founders of Google, Sergey Brin and Larry Page, tracked the progress of ideas that came from them and those that came from others within the organisation and discovered that a greater success rate came from the ideas that came from elsewhere in the organisation and not from the two founders.

Leaders in businesses need to decrease the fear of failure, which means celebrating it as much as celebrating success. Creating a culture where happy, or serendipitous, accidents can happen is vital for innovation to thrive. In fact, former Time Warner chairman, Steve Ross, thought that people who didn't make enough mistakes

[4]'Inner Work Life: Understanding the Subtext of Business Performance', Teresa M. Amabile and Steven J. Kramer, *Harvard Business Review*, May 2007.

[5]'Creativity and the Role of the Leader', Teresa M. Amabile and Mukti Khaire, *Harvard Business Review*, October 2008.

shouldn't be rewarded for not screwing up, they should be fired for not taking enough risks! (See Chapter 12 for more on why accidents should be encouraged at work.)

Matthew Warchus, the film and theatre director, talked to Business Playground about how when directing a production he tries to creates an environment where the fear of failure is reduced: 'I've learnt there are two kinds of bad rehearsal rooms,' he says. 'One is with too much thinking, and one is with too much play, and because the strange thing about my job and putting a show together is that it requires an equal amount of play and thought, one can't move forward without the other stepping in. What you have to do is zigzag between thought and play. In a conventional rehearsal room, for a week or two people would be sitting around a table discussing and then you'd reach the inevitable point when you'd have to stand up and start staging some of these things. That's a point that causes a lot of anxiety for people crossing that threshold, a lot of tension.

'People get too secure with the idea of just talking and thinking, and not with the idea of playing. But, instead, I always make sure that we stand up on the first day. So we'll talk for maybe two or three hours about working on the script and the ideas for it, but before that day is finished we've stood up and just played with one of the scenes, or an idea or a song or something like that, because it removes the threat of that moment. The longer you put it off, the more daunting it gets. But also it puts fluidity into the rehearsal room, it puts mercury in. You get flow, an energy. Obviously you can do that by just people standing around and laughing, but you get a much more important thing which is people just feeling a freedom to get things wrong, to make a fool of themselves, to just go off at a tangent. It becomes a chaotic space, which is much more creative than a formal space.' The lesson for business is to not wait too long before trying out, or prototyping, in some form an idea or innovation you're working on before the fear of failure gets too daunting.

Matthew described to Business Playground how he keeps the process moving when large numbers of people are involved. 'There are a lot of things that I do at the beginning of rehearsals that could be done by anybody in any situation. The thing about talking to lots of people, it's a difficult thing. If I'm doing an opera, or a musical or a movie, there'll be occasions when I turn up and I need to speak to 200 people at the same time and get them to do something, and at times like that you can't allow a democratic thing to take place. Whereas when there are 3 people in a room, each of them can come up with 10 ideas in the space of the meeting, if there are 200 people involved in making a movie, by the time they'd all said their one idea you've run out of time to make the movie. I try to make sure I've expressed whatever my vision is about that scene or about the thing we're trying to do, the scene change, or whatever it is. I get on a microphone and talk to everybody as if I was just talking to one person to say, "Inside my head, this is what I see, and hopefully this will explain why I'm asking you to try this. But, if this doesn't work I'll ask you to try something else in order to try and get the same thing in my head." So I've found that when people know what production they're in, when they know what the vision is for the thing, they're happy. It bonds them together.'

BUILDING BLOCKS

There's usually something positive to say about every idea. Try doing this: whenever you hear an idea, start by saying, 'What I like about this idea is …' and come up with at least one thing that is good about it. The left side of the brain, the cold analytical half, is often too keen to jump in and start editing and thinking of practicalities before the right side has had a proper chance to do its mojo. So, finding positives first means the left side will have to wait a while, drumming its fingers on the table. It gives the idea a chance to breathe and also makes the person who came up with the idea feel good and willing to share ideas in future.

Hi Dave,

Eventually tracked down your email address. I was surprised but delighted that you invited anyone to email you with an issue and this one is probably a corker, given the subject matter of my business. I sell a garden mulch called Strulch! Four years later I am trying to think of new ways to promote it. I started by recruiting 'champions' who would recommend it; it has been on garden TV and in the press and sales are growing slowly but surely. There is only me in the business on a daily basis. Any suggestions would be great.

I enjoyed doing the song and you were very different to what I knew about you. It was a great session, thank you.

Kind regards
Jackie Whiteley
Strulch Limited
(Silver Award Winner Business Link
Bucking The Trend Competition 2009,
Yorkshire Woman of Achievement 2009)

Dear Jackie,

How about shooting a time-lapse (very speeded up) two-minute film of stuff growing rapidly from nothing to beautiful greens and bright colours? Then add in a sexy, sultry female voice-over saying: 'What you are witnessing is the magnificent effects of blah blah blah making everything grow and blossom etc ...' Then the voice changes and says in a giggly playful voice, 'All this because I used Strulch!' You could do this for less than a few hundred pounds on video camera and edit it on a laptop. Just make sure the voice is sexy and warm and rich and recorded really well in a good studio. At the end of the little film drop a bag of Strulch into the shot and include your website info. Put this as any embedded link on every gardening blog in the UK and, of course, on YouTube, etc., with as many tag lines as possible on the theme of sexy gardens, tools, growth, flowers, etc. It should be sexy and funny and will get the point across with humour and get people talking about it.

Cheers
Dave

Ideas can be built up so the positives from each one are combined through a technique known as *successive element integration*,[6] but being simpler folk we're going to call it *building with blocks*. Here's how it works. You start with a bunch of small ideas and add them together to create a more interesting, and developed, bigger idea. Take one idea and add it to a second idea to form a third idea. Then add another idea to the third idea to form a fourth, and so on. For example, to alleviate traffic congestion in LA:

IDEA 1
Make all lanes car pool lanes.[7]

IDEA 2
Build more roads.

Add ideas 1 and 2 together to get a third idea:

IDEA 3
Build whole roads, not just lanes, for people who car pool.

Take another idea from the bunch, such as:

IDEA 4
Improve public transport.

And add this one to Idea 3, to make a new idea:

IDEA 5
Charge people who don't car pool and use the money to fund better public transport.

OK, now the stack of blocks is getting pretty high, but let's see if we can add one more from the pile before it topples over.

IDEA 6
Ask businesses to incentivise employees to car pool.

And add this to the previous idea:

IDEA 7
Suggest businesses put on luxury minibuses for employees to travel to work in the car pool lane, that have wi-fi and coffee so they can start work before they even get to the office.

[6]**www.mycoted.com/Successive_Element_Integration**

[7]Traffic lanes for vehicles carrying two or more passengers.

This last idea ended up being an idea that combined the best bits of lots of ideas, such as how to encourage car pooling and the role businesses can play in this. We might have got to the same solution in other ways, but by accepting that each idea plays some role it means it is a collaborative process that all participants will feel ownership in. Time for a group hug.

MOVE ONE SPACE FORWARD TO THE NEXT CHAPTER ... OR ROLL THE DICE

Trying to be creative without the help of others is not only lonely but also, in a world in which technology has broken down the walls, being able to play well with others is a necessary part of business life. Granted, coming up with ideas through groupthink isn't always easy but, if there is the right spirit of collaboration, the results can be worth it. Having the right team leadership makes all the difference between the good and the plain ugly when it comes to creative collaboration (in fact, a team leader's negative behaviours have way more impact than any good behaviours can ever have and can knock the creative stuffing out of you). Good leaders, like theatre and film director Matthew Warchus, know when to look for new ideas and when not to, in which case they communicate a vision and help their team understand their role in making it happen. Now we've talked about the benefits of a bit of collaboration to create and build ideas, let's take a look ways to expand the possibilities of our thinking, far, far out ...

Instructions

1. Players (the more the merrier) agree on a problem to crack.

2. Each player writes down ideas on a sheet of paper and after two minutes passes them to the player on the left.

3. Now, on the paper, write down new ideas triggered by the first ones.

4. Keep going, passing the ideas on to your neighbour every two minutes, until the paper you started comes all the way back to you, chock full of ideas.

5. Now take turns reading out all of the ideas.

6. Everyone votes and hugs and the winner is the player who came up with the best idea (but in this game love is more important than winning).

BOARD GAME: ALL TOGETHER NOW

How it works: Remember that game Chinese Whispers? (it's called Telephone in the US, probably because the quality of the lines is so bad there), a game based on the old stereotype that Chinese is incomprehensible.[8] You whisper a phrase to the next person, who whispers it to the next, and so on until it comes back to you. By the time it arrives in your ear the phrase is likely to bear no resemblance to how it started. 'The girl with the red hair is wearing a custard-coloured dress' has become 'A large meteor has just landed on my caravan' or something.

How to play: Four or more players agree on a creative challenge and then each comes up with ideas to solve it and writes them down on a piece of paper, leaving enough room for others to add new ideas below. After two minutes they pass their ideas to their neighbour on their left who try to come up with new ideas triggered by the original ones. And so on, passing the pieces of paper to the left every two minutes until they end up back where they started. Players now take turns reading what's on their sheets of paper and the other players vote on which ideas are the best. Players each have 6 points to award: 3 for their favourite idea; 2 for their second favourite; and 1 point for their third favourite.

How to win: The player who came up with the idea that received the most votes.

[8]We've no idea what Chinese Whispers is called in China.

CHAPTER EIGHT
FAR OUT

Think BIG and don't let the truth get in the way of a good story.

Canadian Kyle MacDonald had a pretty unusual idea for how to use a paperclip. He set himself the challenge of seeing what he could get for it by trading-up and, after 14 trades, exactly one year later he ended up with a house in Kipling, Saskatchewan (and that was *before* the housing market crashed in 2007). Kyle told us how he came up with the idea: 'I was bored and I remembered a game called Bigger or Better. **You start with a small object and trade it for a bigger or better object. Repeat. Usually a kids' game. More knocking on doors, less Internet. The red paperclip was the first thing I saw when I thought of the idea.'**

He started on 12 July 2005, by advertising the red paperclip on **www.Craigslist.org**, saying he wanted something bigger and better for it (we like his honest approach) and was offered a fish-shaped pen (this is Canada, after all). He exchanged the pen for a ceramic knob, and in turn: a camping stove, a generator, a beer keg and Budweiser sign, a snowmobile, a trip to the Canadian Rockies, a supply truck and a recording contract. Next, in April 2006, he got a year's rent in a flat in Phoenix.

Then it gets really weird. He got a lot of publicity, ended up as a bit of celebrity and was contacted by a Hollywood actor, Corbin Bernsen (from TV series *LA Law*). Kyle told us he thinks Corbin might have been bored too and the idea just appealed to him. He then traded his Phoenix flat for an afternoon with Alice Cooper. Eh? According to Kyle's blog, 'Alice Cooper is a gold mine of awesomeness and fun.' And he traded that afternoon of fun for a snow globe of the band KISS. Now, it seems actor Bernsen was a collector of snow globes, so wily Kyle used the KISS orb as bait and asked readers of his blog to send more globes to Bernsen in exchange for signed photographs of him, Bernsen and the KISS globe. Kyle ended up getting a movie role from Bernsen to barter. Publicity-hungry Kipling (a town with a population of 1,140, thought to be named after Rudyard) decided that it could benefit from Kyle's quest, so it bought an unoccupied house (worth about $45,000 at the time) and offered it to him in exchange for the movie part. They planned to hold a contest to audition for the role. According to Kyle's blog, the town's revised offer to him went something like this:

'Kyle, the Town of Kipling, Saskatchewan, wants you to complete your quest for a house. The Mayor and Town Council, with the support of the employees and residents of the Town of Kipling, have a revised offer for you. We know you will say Yes!

1   As a new resident to our community you will receive a Community Welcome Package containing local information and promotions from local businesses.

2   The Kipling Chamber of Commerce will give you $200 in Kipling Cash. This Cash can be spent at any local Chamber of Commerce business.

3   You will be given a Key to the Town of Kipling.

4   You will become Honorary Mayor of Kipling for One Day.

5   You will be named an Honorary Lifelong Citizen of the Town of Kipling.

6   The day we make the trade will be decreed One Red Paperclip Day by our Town Council and everyone will be encouraged to wear a red paperclip in honor of your achievements.

7   We will build the world's largest red paperclip in dedication to you and your 'one red paperclip project'.

8   Most importantly, to allow you to complete your quest … We will trade to you a house. The house was built in the 1920s and has been recently renovated. It is locate at 503 Main Street Kipling, SK, Canada. It is approximately 1,100 square feet on two floors. There are three bedrooms, one and a half bathrooms, kitchen, living room and dining room. It has white vinyl siding, a new roof and eaves troughs that have been put on in the last few years. We will be sending you pictures of the house as soon as we have had time to touch up the paint.

Kyle MacDonald, do you accept our offer of one house in Kipling for one role in Corbin Bernsen's movie *Donna on Demand*?'

Kyle accepted and the deal was done on 12 July 2006. The movie *Donna in Demand* was released in 2008, featuring Kipling resident Nolan Hubbard who had won the audition for the part.

For a while you could go to Kyle's website[1] and make an offer for the house, and more than one person offered a red paperclip for it, but he eventually donated the house back to the town of Kipling. And what has the whole experience taught Kyle? He told Business Playground: 'If you don't take the first step, you'll never go anywhere.'

IT WAS HOW BIG?!

Dramatisation when used as a tool to solve problems creatively can force us to think a little bigger. The thing is, **we tend to have mindsets that are in proportion to the size of the problem: if it seems smallish, we'll think small, if it looks BIG, we'll think a little bigger, and if a challenge has crisis proportions we'll apply all our creative energies to getting it solved.** Think of how the language around climate change shifted over time from the cutesy and benign 'global warming' to the much more dramatic, and accurate, 'climate crisis'. Al Gore started using the words 'climate crisis' because he'd been told by his advisors that the problem wouldn't be seen as particularly harmful or urgent otherwise (other polls indicated that 'crisis' was too dramatic, and that 'climate change' might strike the right balance and shake people out of their complacency). In the introduction to his 2006 book *An Inconvenient Truth*[2] he states, 'The climate crisis is, indeed, extremely dangerous. In fact it is a true planetary emergency.'

[1] www.oneredpaperclip.com

[2] *An Inconvenient Truth: The Planetary Emergency of Global Warming and What We Can Do About It*, Al Gore, Rodale Books, 2006.

Al Gore understood that until he could get people to see the scale of the problem they would be unwilling to take it seriously enough to change their behaviour.

Other experts have used the term 'global heating' to communicate the idea that it's about getting hot, not just warm. Dr Lovelock, environmental expert and author of the brilliant 2006 book *Revenge of Gaia: Earth's Climate Crisis and the Fate of Humanity*, has said,[3] 'Warming is something that's kind of cozy and comfortable. You think of a nice duvet on a cold winter's day. Heating is something you want to get away from.' Meanwhile, opponents to the idea that mankind is having an adverse effect on the planet's climate have tried to give the problem much milder labels. Language expert and Republican Party consultant Frank Luntz wrote a memo in 2002 that advised the party to use the term 'climate change', rather than 'global warming'. In the memo he wrote: '"Climate change" is less frightening than "global warming".[4] As one focus group participant noted, climate change "Sounds like you're going from Pittsburgh to Fort Lauderdale." While global warming has catastrophic connotations attached to it, climate change suggests a more controllable and less emotional challenge.' Before the memo, Bush used the term 'global warming' frequently in public speeches, but subsequently hardly at all.[5] Luntz wrote in his memo, 'A compelling story, even if factually inaccurate, can be more emotionally compelling than a dry recitation of the truth.'

[3]It's ironic that on one side of the debate, 'global warming' was seen to be too mild a term and 'climate change' the more urgent and therefore better term, and on the other the opposite was true. So 'climate change' ended up being recommended by some advisors on both sides, but for exact opposite reasons.

[4]'Global Heating, Atmosphere Cancer, Pollution Death. What's in a Name?', Andrew C. Revkin, **www.nytimes.com**

[5]'Memo Exposes Bush's New Green Strategy', Oliver Burkeman, the *Guardian*, 4 March 2003.

Similarly, John F. Kennedy knew what he was doing in May 1961 when he created a crisis for America by announcing to the nation they must win the space race against the Soviets or lose their place as the world's dominant nation. And, lo just over eight years later, on 20 July 1969, the United States of America became the first nation to put men on the moon. Kennedy had said in a speech to a joint session of Congress: 'Recognising the head start obtained by the Soviets with their large rocket engines, which gives them many months of lead time, and recognising the likelihood that they will exploit this lead for some time to come in still more impressive successes, we nevertheless are required to make new efforts. For while we cannot guarantee that one day we shall be first, we can guarantee that any failure to make this effort will find us last.'

People tend to think of more innovative solutions when given a bigger problem to solve. It stops your thinking being in small increments and allows you to dream up big ideas that are very different in nature and scale. How can you dramatise your own business challenge so you focus creative energy in the right direction? How could you bring it to life to inspire yourself and other stakeholders to crack it?

How about a bit of exaggeration to make the point? This is without doubt the best business book ever written; it'll change your life and solve the world's problems too. Oh, and it's completely edible and nutritious and makes for a very tasty meal. Exaggeration is a wonderful thing. No, actually, it's the best thing ever, ever, EVER. Remember our ball-gazing technique of Chapter 3, and how thinking up what might seem like crazy future scenarios can free us from our mental shackles? No? Well, anyway, our point is that exaggerating a scenario to extreme proportions is also a great way to get the creative juices flowing. With our *too much traffic congestion in LA* example, an exaggeration of the situation (though not too much of one) would be that cars are absolutely stationary in LA. There is absolute gridlock. People can't get to work. They can't make their ways home. Pregnant women can't reach hospitals. Michael Douglas leaves his car in the middle of the jammed street. (Oh, sorry that's a movie,[6] but it's also scarily real, and you get the idea. Nothing is moving.) A solution to this exaggerated scenario might be to quit using cars altogether. It might be impractical, but the notion might free up some ideas for ways to dramatically reduce the number of cars on the roads that otherwise we might not have considered.[7]

MAD WORLD

While in business the temptation is to try to maintain control as much as possible, it is often a liberating and fruitful experience to think of the most outlandish ideas you can and then work on ways to make them practical. **When trying to come up with creative solutions we need to ignore the most obvious ones, or at least put them to one side with a reassuring 'there, there, just wait quietly here' pat on the head.** Obvious solutions are likely too similar to what the situation is already like now and won't take you anywhere meaningful and new (see the *Chaos Theory* section in Chapter 10).

You can make it into a game. Gather together a small group of people and sell them numbered cards for a pound each. Write up the problem on a board or piece of paper and give them ten minutes to write down on their cards the most unlikely solution they can think of for the problem, one idea per card. Players then look at each

[6]*Falling Down* (1993).

[7]Or at the other extreme, minimise the problem so actually it doesn't seem like much of one at all. Make it very, very tiny. Then the solutions would take more of a positive spin and be about ways to make the most of the situation, not try to radically alter it. Find you're spending a little tiny bit longer in the car than you'd want to? No problem, have some fun while you're there. There could be a radio station dedicated to people stuck in LA traffic with local news and gossip, or a series of self-improvement CDs or podcasts in bite-sized pieces that turn the delay into a useful experience. Rather than try to radically alter the situation, we have now accepted it and made the best of it.

June 2009

Dave,

I have asked my father if he could forward you a mail after seeing your amazing performance at the conference. I found it extremely funny, informative and way ahead of its time. The lesbian grandma chocolate advert made me cry I laughed so much.

I have a café-bar in Leeds called The Roast Café. We are situated on the river, have a good terraced area and relaxed friendly decor (Paul Smith-type stripes on doors, herbs in the windows, goldfish, different types of seat covers, burgundy Chesterfields and the staff wear Fred Perrys). We are open for breakfast (15 per cent of the business), lunch (45 per cent of the business) and dinner serving British-style food (10 per cent of the business); from great bacon butties and chicken Caesar salads to John Dory with samphire[8] and sundried tomatoes. I have attached our evening menu for you to have a look at. The evening side of the business could deliver us so much more profit if marketed with a difference. We also do outside catering to offices for meetings (30 per cent of the business) and host events at the venue. Breakfast and lunch are very successful, the evenings have proved to be more difficult despite mentions in *Vogue* and other good write-ups. The evening food is as good as the best restaurants in Leeds.

My question is do you have any ideas how to drive our event business, targeting individuals, companies (despite all their budgets being slashed) and party organisers within the Leeds area? If that requires marketing the whole venue in a different way, so that we become better known, then I will give it a go. We have very limited budgets, but would give anything a go. I am well into purple cows and any other things you could come up with. If you could help I would really appreciate it.

Cheers,
Matthew Firth
Roast Café

[8]A type of edible plant.

Dear Matthew,

Did you ever hear of 'The House of Blues' in the USA? They created something called the Gospel Brunch that was totally unique and a massive success with Sunday lunchtime queues around the block.

www.houseofblues.com/venues/clubvenues/
gospelbrunch.php

I think if you create a unique event that involves eating and an uplifting thing it will work. Also in USA they have a thing called 'a roast' where people get together and honour one person, but they 'roast' him or her, all tell stories and send him or her up. Do they do that in the UK? That could be a perfect fit!

Dave

other's cards and add notes to the crazy ideas for ways to make them more practical. A crazy solution for reducing traffic congestion might be to get everyone to fly instead. Another player might add to this idea, as a way to make the original implausible idea plausible, that there could be short shuttle flights between different local LA airports (e.g. LAX, Burbank, Santa Monica and Long Beach).

Once everyone has had a chance to add their suggestions to the ideas, they each have two votes to give to the two ideas they consider now to be the most implausible. These are the ones for which the additions didn't help bring them back to earth much. The idea with the most votes for being the most implausible wins all the money! In other words, the craziest idea is rewarded rather than the most practical one, so forcing people to think outlandishly. But along the way the ideas that didn't win might have some real potential as practical solutions to the problem. Sneaky, huh? **Now get those obvious ideas out of the corner and send them home.**

A variation on this is to split the group into two teams. Each team comes up with an unlikely solution to the problem and the other has to add some suggestions to it to make it more realistic. If a team makes the opposing team's idea more feasible then they get a point (or a doughnut, or whatever) and if not, the doughnut goes to the other greedy sods.

O SUPERMAN[9]

In the 1978 film, *Superman*, baddie Lex Luther gives Superman two big problems to solve, knowing full well Superman only has time to do one. The first is a nuclear missile heading full tilt to the San Andreas Fault that will cause an earthquake in California, the other a missile aimed at Hackensack, New Jersey. Superman opts to save New Jersey, and in the aftershock of the earthquake caused by the Californian missile Lois Lane's car falls into a crevice, earth falls on top of her and she dies. Not a good Hollywood ending. So Superman will have to bring Lois back to life. What does he do? What any one of us would do if we were a superhero, he alters the course of history by spinning the Earth in the opposite direction from its normal course, so reversing the time to before when she died, allowing him to save her.

Superheroes, as we all know, have super powers – hence their name. So, what if we could apply those powers to the problem we're trying to solve? Let's get together a group of ordinary mortals and make them into superheroes. They can either pick who they want to be or can be randomly assigned their new roles. Here's our set of superheroes, but you can make up your own.

People can even be given props to help them to get into character. Now they can apply their superpowers to the problem.

[9] *O Superman (for Massenet)* is an experimental song written by Laurie Anderson in 1981 and is part of the much larger work, *United States*. Anderson married long-time companion Lou Reed in 1981.

Dirk Digglertron – has the power to make things VERY BIG.

Porschedriver – has the power to make things very small.

Madoff – has the power to make things (like large amounts of money) disappear.

The Politician – has the power to s-t-r-e-t-c-h t-h-i-n-g-s.

The Telekinesist – has the power to transport things instantly.

Duploid – has the power to double things.

The Bulk – has incredible strength.

Mindbender – has incredible powers of hypnosis.

Viagratro – has the power to make things levitate.

For traffic congestion in LA *The Telekinesist* might use his powers of transportation to instantly take all the cars out of the city. **How might we do a similar thing in real life, without resorting to superpowers?** Maybe not all the cars, but at least some of them. Should we, for instance, only allow certain types of cars on the roads, such as ones with high fuel efficiency?

Duploid might double the number of cars on the road to make the traffic situation in the city so intolerable that it forces commuters to leave their cars at home and think of alternatives. In real life we could find other ways, penalties for instance, to encourage people to rely less on their cars. Or if *Duploid* were feeling more benign he might double the number of buses, so making it easier for people to use public transport, and so we might then start thinking of ideas to increase the number of buses in the city.

And, of course, the powerful *Viagratro* could use his powers of levitation to raise cars off the ground, leaving those left on roads to travel around more freely. And this idea might get us thinking about how overhead rail systems do a similar thing, like literally raising people off the ground in cars (although those ones stay up for more than a couple of hours).

MOVE ONE SPACE FORWARD TO THE NEXT CHAPTER ... OR ROLL THE DICE

This chapter has been about how thinking BIG can help trigger interesting ideas. Kyle MacDonald wanted to see how far he could go by starting with a single red paperclip, and after a series of barter trades he ended up with a three-bedroom house in Saskatchewan, Canada. Evocative language can help us think big by dramatising a problem and bringing it to life (and, on the other hand, language can also be used to make it not seem like much of a problem at all). **When trying to come up with creative solutions we need to use whatever tricks we can to fire up the imagination, like exaggeration for instance.** Exaggeration can lead to thinking that takes us away from the more obvious solutions and allows our imagination to run a little wild. Now in the next chapter let's investigate what looking at things from people's different perspectives, or trying on their shoes, can do.

START

Instructions

1. Come up with ideas for things to do with a paperclip.
2. At the back of the book there's a list of ideas people often say.
3. Move one space for every idea you came up with that's also on the list, but two spaces for every idea that isn't on the list.
4. The longest chain of paperclips wins!

BOARD GAME: FAR OUT

How it works: Kyle MacDonald thought of a quite amazing use for a paperclip – trade it for a house. It was a pretty far out idea and not something you'd normally come up with as a use for a paperclip. This game is about thinking up other interesting ideas for how to use a paperclip.

How to play: Players create the longest chain of paperclips that they can by coming up with ideas for things to do with a paperclip. Find a paperclip to use as a counter and see how many spaces you can move along the board. On page 235 there is a list of ideas that people given the task will typically come up. Move one space along the board for every idea already on the list, but two whole paperclips for every idea not included on the list.

How to win: You're playing against yourself so everyone's a winner. Just see how far you can get around the board.

CHAPTER NINE
SHOE SWAPPER

Looking at
problems
from different
perspectives.

INEXPERT WITNESSES

On 20 June 1913 William Marconi, inventor of the radio, sat in court rapt by the testimony of an expert witness in a lawsuit that his Marconi Wireless Telegraph Company of America had brought against the National Electric Signaling Company of Pittsburg. Marconi sat next to his wife and, according to a *New York Times* story that day, 'Both listened attentively to every word spoken by Frank L. Waterman, an experts in patents and regarded as an authority on matters relating to wireless telegraphy.' A lot hung on what Waterman was saying. At issue was whether the Pittsburg dudes had infringed wireless technology patents Marconi had filed in 1896 and were making money from his ideas. Waterman, supporting Marconi's claim that he and he alone should have claim to sole use of the patent rights, said in his testimony that Marconi had not only made wireless practicable but also made it a commercial reality.[1]

Expert witnesses like Frank Waterman are brought in to offer advice in court cases because there is a need for the specialised knowledge they possess. Their knowledge of the subject matter enlightens the judge and jury, enabling them to form a more complete and accurate opinion of a subject that is relevant to the case. We don't know how much Frank was paid for his expertise, but nowadays good experts in the US can make thousands for their time and knowledge. (According to one US study of the matter, the average hourly rate is $300 although, perhaps bizarrely, the less-experienced experts tend to charge more than experienced ones.[2])

[1]Mrs Marconi told reporters, 'I think he will win, and I think he ought to. I believe that a man who obtains a patent on his ideas is the man who deserves all the credit for what those ideas have accomplished rather than a person who improves on the patent.' She was right and Marconi won, proving Mr Waterman's value as an expert witness, but she ended up being wrong in the long term. After years of legal battles, in 1943 the US Supreme Court overturned most of Marconi's patents. It should be noted that at the time the US Government was involved in its own patent dispute with Marconi, leading some observers to suggest the Supreme Court ruling was biased.

[2]From 'SEAK, Inc. National Guide to Expert Witness Fees and Billing Procedures'.

We are all expert witnesses to some extent, in that we have specialised knowledge in some area or another. Expertise that can be very useful in the way it helps us define the creative challenge, filter our ideas and implement the ones that have the greatest chance of success. On the other hand, expertise can also get in the way of idea generation and knowing too much can positively inhibit the creative process. **We know the rules, we know what's been done before, we know what works and what doesn't work and therefore *we think* we know what we shouldn't even bother trying. And often we're wrong.** As co-founder of Intel, Andrew Grove said in a 2005 interview: 'When everybody knows that something is so, it means that nobody knows nothin'.' He believes the best way to tackle a problem is to set aside everything you already know.[3]

A research study[4] looked at how what we think we know colours our perceptions. People were randomly assigned as either *tappers* or *listeners*. The tappers had to tap out well-known songs with their knuckles, such as *Happy Birthday to You* or the *Star-Spangled Banner*, while the listeners had to try and identify them. Results showed that because the tappers knew what the songs were, they assumed that the listeners would easily get them from the rhythm they were tapping out on the tabletop. They estimated that the listeners would correctly name about half of the songs. In fact, they only got right 2.5 per cent, a twentieth of that number. The *Journal of Political Economy* described as 'the curse of knowledge' the condition of how once you're an expert in a particular field it's difficult to imagine not knowing what you know.

[3]'Innovative Minds Don't Think Alike', Janet Rae-Dupree, *The New York Times*, 30 December 2007.

[4]'Overconfidence in the Communication of Intent: Heard and Unheard Melodies', an unpublished doctoral dissertation by Elizabeth Newton, Stanford University, 1990.

We advocate bringing in *in*expert witnesses to offer a fresh perspective on the creative problems we're trying to solve. Witnesses unencumbered by too much experience or too many rules, who don't know what's been tried and what hasn't. These *inexperts* could be people from within the organisation who work in a different discipline and have little or no familiarity with the area being worked on, or people even further removed from the business – for instance, roofers, writers, musicians, sushi chefs or jockeys – who can help look at the problem through fresh pairs of eyes and reveal a whole new perspective you might not have previously considered.

Of course, the freshest eyes to bring in are those who are removed from business life altogether – children. **A child's perspective is by definition naïve and so hasn't yet been tainted by the rules of business and marketplace.** If you can find a very simple and clear way to explain your challenge it can be very worthwhile asking some kids you know for some ideas, perhaps by asking the help of a teacher and making it into a class project (what, for instance, might a class of five-year-old kids suggest as solutions to a problem such as too much traffic?) and use what they come up with as a method of looking at the problem in a totally fresh way. An added benefit is that most children don't charge such big hourly fees.

"I'm a hopeless enthusiast, not just for my own ventures but for everyone else's too! I've been diagnosed as manic-depressive, except without the depressive bit. I can't stop and, who cares, I'm having fun. Sometimes I think some people don't know what they know. In other words, they've put their knowledge into such a small context and imagine that is the only use for it.

For instance, I was once in a black cab in London. I always chat to the cab driver or the petrol pump attendant, or the chap filling the mini bar in the hotel room, or basically anyone who wants to chat during the day. But this time it was the cab driver. He was telling me that things had changed and he didn't like driving the cab any more. I was asking him what the problem was and he said that now there were too many drunks and aggressive people, and the streets were too crowded and all the charm of being a cabbie had gone for him.

Now, these drivers have to go through very complicated and rigorous testing to get 'The Knowledge' as they call it. So I said, 'Hey, why don't you stop and do something else?'. And he said that it was impossible because it was all he knew how to do. He was thinking, 'This is all I know.' I thought for a second and said, 'But you know so much about London, all the streets and the ups and downs of cab driving and judging people's temperament and how to stay safe, etc. etc. Why don't you make it into a board game? How to get from A to B on time in rush hour, and avoiding getting a ticket or picking up a drunk on a Saturday night. Write everything you know and then make a kind of 'Snakes and Ladders' or 'Monopoly'-type game out of it. Give it a name, register it and then meet with a game company.

We had a good old discussion about this and then he dropped me off at my house at Wychcombe Studios in Hampstead, London. About two years later there was knock at the door at my same house, and my wife at the time, Siobhan, answered. She came into the kitchen and said some guy was there, said he was taxi driver and he had something to give me. Yep, it was the game and he had a game company that had produced it for him and he was now a royalty-receiving game inventor! You see, sometimes 'You Don't Know What You Know'."

DO YOU WANNA BE IN MY GANG?

Imagine there's a gang of kids (*Famous Five* or *Swallows and Amazons* type kids, not the mean ones from *Lord of the Flies*) who all hang out together and go on adventures.

The dynamics between the gang members are interesting; they argue about things but always try to find common ground. When there are differences of opinion different members of the gang might form little allegiances. Naoki and Arata might team up to passionately argue their case against Ryota, Bunko and Shiori, or boys might be on one side and girls on another, but regardless they always work together as one to deal with any outside enemy.

So how might Naoki, Ryota, Arata, Shiori and Bunko approach a problem differently? Naoki would be trying to find solutions that take into account the feelings of as many of the gang members and the people they come into contact with as possible. Shiori would be thinking very broadly about the problem and the other areas it might be associated with. Ryota would be focused on finding a solution quickly rather than pondering too much if it's the right one. Bunko would take the opposite approach, wanting to explore every avenue before coming to a conclusion. And Arata would be hell-bent on coming up with a solution that nobody had tried before and be more interested in the unknown nature of it than the results.

All of the gang members have something to offer. Each of their perspectives and ways of doing things has some merit, and imagining how they each might approach a problem can help us switch into different modes of solving it. We can try to imagine what each of them might think and then, when we have some ideas, think about which would agree with each solution, what arguments might ensue and how we might reconcile them. Is there one that is radical enough for Arata, yet doesn't upset Naoki's status quo? Can it fit the facts enough for Bunko and still not lose Shiori's interest by being too rooted in reality? And can it be made to happen without too much dilly-dallying so Arata feels like things are actually getting done? Soon to be a major motion picture …

Naoki, the sensitive one, is very aware of his own and other people's feelings and is always thinking what somebody meant by what they said or did. He's quick to laugh and quick to tears and is always trying to restore balance and harmony in the group.

Shiori, the daydreamer, just goes with the flow and often seems to be in another world. She can often be found wandering around at the edge of the other's activities, not quite a part of them. She will often say something profound and seemingly unconnected to what's going on, and only later will others realise what she meant by it.

Ryota, the leader, is self-assured and bossy. He likes to feel in control and will always make the final decision on what the gang should do. He acts and reacts quickly without thinking things through too much and his decisiveness means they get things done, but can also lead the gang into trouble.

Bunko, the brainy one, is very fact-based and analytical. She loves to think through problems and come up with the most logical solutions based on the facts. She is loud and will challenge Ryota if she thinks he's going about something the wrong way, and she can upset Naoki by her blunt, commonsense opinions.

Arata, the rebellious one, is the one most likely to get the group into scrapes because he's always pushing boundaries, but that means he's also the one most likely to push them into exciting adventures. He hates accepting things because that's the way things are and is apt to go off on his own if he gets too bored with the group.

I was incredibly creative when I was a child, driving my parents nuts. I was full of schemes to make some pocket money, but never went about them in a regular way. I watched boys delivering newspapers and getting paid, but I could see you needed a bicycle or it was lot of work and a very heavy bag to carry. I decided that to sell newspapers was good, but to carry a heavy bag around was bad.

So I asked at the newsagent where the newspapers came from and they told me the address of the local distributor. Then I went down there and somehow negotiated to have a whole heap of Sunday newspapers delivered to me in a bus shelter on Kayll Road. I'd seen that this bus shelter was very busy on Sunday mornings with men coming home from nightshifts and it was on a corner surrounded by four streets of houses.

I had ten times more papers than anyone could carry but it didn't matter because I was just sitting on them! I would sell out in a few hours and go back to the wholesaler and pay him his amount and end up keeping five times more money than if I had had a paper round carrying those heavy papers in a sack every morning – and I only had to do a few hours' work. Then I added another element. I took my guitar and started busking to the bus queue as well, which earned me a few more pounds on top. But the coup de grâce was when I started hiring my own paper boys to deliver locally and then asked my dad if he could run the business as it was getting too much for me – at 12 years old! This worked out for a couple of Sundays. I had my dad running the stall, paperboys delivering the papers and I was having a lie-in on a Sunday morning. Needless to say, the novelty soon wore off for my dad (who had a full-time job), so I sold the business on.

This wasn't the only business idea I had as a kid. I had endless fun thinking of new ones. One of my favourites was when I bought an old electric-shock machine and I would charge a penny a shock, guaranteeing my classmates it would give them energy and make them more intelligent to help them pass a test.

I always liked the creative shortcut to a problem. So when I realised, at around 14 years old, that I could write a song, I thought, OK, so how do I get people to hear it? So I went to my dad's telephone directory and looked up radio stations. I saw Radio Durham and I knew this was the university town and students might like the songs I was writing. So I called them. 'Hello, Radio Durham,' said a very bright-sounding female.

'Hi,' I said, 'I've written some songs and I want to play and sing them on your radio station.' And before she could answer I said, 'Here, I'll play one now,' and I put down the receiver and started strumming and singing, completely forgetting how long this was taking.

Anyway, after about five minutes I picked up the phone again and said, 'Did you like it?' There was silence for a while and she said, 'Yes, it was very good, but I'm the receptionist.' I said, 'That's OK, just tell the others and call me back,' and gave her my number.

About a week later I was watching the *Beverly Hillbillies* on TV around 5.30p.m. and the phone rang. My dad came in the room looking confused and saying, 'Radio Durham on the phone for you.' I, of course, was completely unfazed. I'd been waiting for them to call back. I'd already visualised me doing four songs in the radio studio and doing an interview and then going on television doing the same in Newcastle.

All of this happened and I got my first cheque for £12 for my radio performance, then another cheque from the TV performance! Now this is a mixture of creative thinking and downright cheek or chutzpah, but it certainly cut out a few years of playing to myself in the bedroom and it was a lot of fun.

I was so into visualisation when I was younger that I would stand outside my house on a summer's day (at the end of a busy shopping street) wearing full skiing gear, goggles, etc., on some homemade wooden skis. It wouldn't bother me that people were staring or kids were calling me names. It made no difference – to me I was already skiing in Austria and with my eyes closed. Six months later I was in Innsbruck in Austria coming second place in the junior slalom.

Now all of this came to an abrupt end when I turned 18 years old. I was now in London, had a record deal and a publishing deal, but I had also discovered drugs. Now, drugs can make you very creative, as is well documented throughout history, but not if you take so many that it takes you all day to make a cup of tea and fry an egg. So I would say for three or four years I didn't really write a song or invent anything much, just ran around trying to get more drugs to help me come down from the other drugs. I know this is meant to be a business book, but I'm now talking about one of the biggest businesses in the world and I was on the receiving end of a well-organised assault on my brain cells. There was disaster after disaster and I went through a bunch of personas ... like, turning up to the studio wearing a kilt and sporran, or walking to the local shop and being reminded by the grocer as he escorted me out that I was actually wearing nothing at all.

It all came to a sticky end when I ended up in hospital after being in a car crash and started having recurring lung collapses. Now, you are thinking, 'Where the hell is this going? I paid good money for this book.' Well, remember earlier I said that electric shocks give you energy and make you smarter? I was about to find out the truth of this, big time, because I was about to die and had the biggest electric shock you ever want to have with defibrillators. I came back to life and, guess what, I've never stopped having ideas since.

Literally since leaving that hospital my whole life changed. I was the old me again: no more drugs. I was inventing new ways to record music, reading everything I could on art and filmmaking, even learning to cook and inventing exotic dishes for Annie and my imaginary friends to try. Actually, dying and being brought back to life was like being plugged into an electric socket that pumps creative energy into your veins! It's better than any drug on the planet and it creates infinite possibilities. We advise the electric-shock treatment and Business Playground is developing one now that you soon might be able to buy for the office.

MOVE ONE SPACE FORWARD TO THE NEXT CHAPTER ... OR ROLL THE DICE

Getting too close to a problem can make it difficult to come up with innovative solutions because we tend to be hampered by what we know, or think we know, about what's likely to work. A research study in which people had to get others to recognise familiar tunes by tapping them out with their knuckles showed how what we already know affects our perceptions and skews our judgement. Whereas, if we look at problems through the eyes of someone else, whether a child or a passenger in a cab, the fresh perspectives can lead to ideas that aren't constrained by old rigid thinking. In business we should solicit views from, or try on the shoes of, *inexperts* who can add something new to the problem: people from different departments or from completely unrelated professions. Now, in the next chapter we'll show you how to throw some other unexpected elements into the mix.

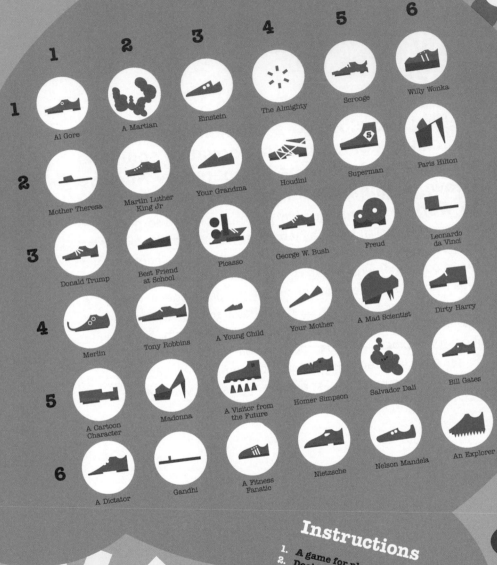

1 **2** **3** **4** **5** **6**

1 Al Gore · A Martian · Einstein · The Almighty · Scrooge · Willy Wonka

2 Mother Theresa · Martin Luther King Jr · Your Grandma · Houdini · Superman · Paris Hilton

3 Donald Trump · Best Friend at School · Picasso · George W. Bush · Freud · Leonardo da Vinci

4 Merlin · Tony Robbins · A Young Child · Your Mother · A Mad Scientist · Dirty Harry

5 A Cartoon Character · Madonna · A Visitor from the Future · Homer Simpson · Salvador Dali · Bill Gates

6 A Dictator · Gandhi · A Fitness Fanatic · Nietzsche · Nelson Mandela · An Explorer

Instructions

1. A game for playing on your lonesome.
2. Decide on a problem to solve and throw a pair of dice to see whose shoes to wear.
3. See how many ideas you can come up with in five minutes.
4. Now swap shoes by throwing the dice again and come up with ideas from the new perspective.
5. The winner is the best idea after three rounds!

BOARD GAME: SHOE SWAPPER

How it works: To get the brain thinking in new directions to solve a creative problem we need go outside what is familiar. We need to experience new things and bring diversity into the mix. In fact, we need to put ourselves into other people's shoes.

How to play: You (yes, you're on your own for this one) try to come up with creative solutions to a chosen problem by taking the perspective of, or putting yourself in the shoes of, different types of people. In each of three rounds you have five minutes to write down ideas from the unique perspectives of the people whose shoes you are wearing.

Example: The problem you're trying to solve might be how to bring more customers into a restaurant. In the first round you throw a 6 and a 2, leading to Paris Hilton's boots.

Now you should generate as many ideas as you can from the perspective of Paris Hilton in five minutes. In Paris's shoes you might think that a great way to drive business for the restaurant would be to offer the clientele celebrity gift bags, and this might spark another idea about making customers at the restaurant feel very special, like a celebrity in fact. There could be a gift bag containing unusual toys and a fake paparazzi photographer stationed at the entrance, and framed on the wall of the restaurant could be autographed photos of celebrity customers.

How to win: Play three rounds and the winner is the idea that best solves the problem.

CHAPTER TEN
CONNECTED

The art of
putting
unconnected
things together
to create
something
completely
new.

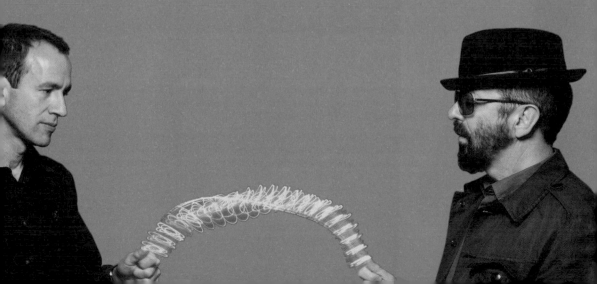

In the late 1950s and early 1960s, novelist and key figure in the Beat Generation William S. Burroughs[1] developed the *cut-up technique*, a method of creative writing in which text is cut up into smaller pieces and then rearranged randomly. In the 1975 BBC documentary about David Bowie, *Cracked Actor*, we see him creating song lyrics by randomly picking phrases he's written on strips of paper. We watch as he cuts a sheet into strips, on which he's some written phrases, and then piece them together, starting with 'I'm an alligator', and next 'I'm a mama papa', forming the lyrics for what becomes his song, *Moonage Daydream*. He explains that he's only used the technique on a couple of songs but has found it helpful igniting what's in his imagination.[2] Kurt Cobain also experimented with the cut-up technique and Thom Yorke, of Radiohead, used it when writing the band's *Kid A* album by writing single lines of lyrics, putting them in a hat and drawing them out randomly to make a song.

While we're not (necessarily) advocating totally giving up control, **when it comes to freeing up some creativity in business there's something to be said for adding a degree of chance.** We believe that some well-orchestrated chaos can be a wonderful thing.[3]

[1]His work includes *Naked Lunch*, and Burroughs' life was fictionalised in Jack Kerouac's *On The Road*. Burroughs said that T.S. Eliot's 434-line poem *The Waste Land* (1922) is an example of the cut-up technique.

[2]*Cracked Actor* is the title of a song released on Bowie's phenomenal 1973 album *Aladdin Sane*. It should be noted that *Moonage Daydream* was written by Bowie in 1971 so we can only assume that in the documentary, which was filmed in 1974, he was recreating how he had written it.

[3]*Recipes for Disaster: An Anarchist Cookbook*, a 624-page manual, described by the editors, CrimethInc. Ex-Workers's Collective, as 'a tactical handbook for revolutionary action', was written collectively over three years and released in 2004. One of the 62 chapters (or 'recipes') is called *Behavioral Cut-Ups*, and involves connecting two unrelated socially-acceptable behaviours, such as public speaking and public transport, to create something new, such as making a speech on a bus.

SLIPPING ON BANANA SKINS

'Humor is reason gone mad.'
Groucho Marx

Is it just us, or is watching someone slipping on a banana skin always funny? You can't help but laugh even though you've seen it a million times (never in real life, unfortunately) and know exactly what's going to happen each time. **Humour and creativity are very closely related.** In fact, creative people are often very funny too. Like creativity, making people laugh often involves making connections between two seemingly unrelated ideas that results in something surprising and different. Take a man walking along the street minding his own business, especially one who is doing something self-absorbed, like reading a newspaper (or checking his email), add an innocuous-looking banana skin and you get a result that is dramatically different from what the pedestrian intended. Arse in air looking stunned (but not seriously hurt, of course – if he ended up breaking his neck, the humour mostly disappears). From in control to helpless and surprised in less than the time it takes to say, 'What the … !'

Slipping on banana skins is more than just funny; it can help the creative process too, especially when the ideas aren't flowing as easily as they should. Throw in a joke or a provocative image and see how that can disrupt thinking that might be becoming stale or getting stuck in a rut. It doesn't really matter what it is so long as it serves the same function as the real banana skin does, by changing the course of what's happening in a dramatic and sudden way. It introduces an element that is bizarre or outrageous or irreverent, and makes an odd connection between two ideas as a way to tell the brain to do the same with the problem it's working on. It's saying to the left side of the brain to step back for a while and let the more freewheeling right side take a shot at it. It's a mental nudge saying it's OK to let loose a little and bring in some more crazy thoughts.

Several studies have found that being funny and being creative are ready bedfellows. One, for instance, way back in 1965, was about the relationship between wit, sarcasm and creativity. Results showed the 'wits' among the 156 airmen being tested to be better than the less witty ones at group problem-solving.[4] Other studies have found a positive correlation between creativity and the ability to comprehend humour (getting the joke) among undergraduates and children, as well as between humour production (making the jokes) and creativity. The researchers argued that the link between humour and creativity is because the two have a common basis in the ability to find hidden connections between apparently disparate concepts.[5] Studies by Avner Ziv (we think his name is an anagram, but can't quite figure out for what) also support this link. In one of them,[6] adolescents who had listened to a funny recording did significantly better on creativity tests than those who had not. In another,[7] Ziv asked adolescents to write witty captions to cartoons or write witty responses to the standard Torrance Creativity Test, and in both cases he found the 'humorous atmosphere' significantly increased their creativity scores.

> **HA + HA = AHA!**

[4]'Wit, Creativity, and Sarcasm', E.E. Smith and H.L. White, *Journal of Applied Psychology*, 49, pp.131–134, 1965.

[5]'Creativity and Sense of Humor', L.L. Rouff, *Psychological Reports*, 37, p.1022. 1975.

[6]'Facilitating Effects of Humor on Creativity', Avner Ziv, *Journal of Educational Psychology*; Vol. 68, No. 3, pp. 318–22, 1976.

[7]'The Influence of Humorous Atmosphere on Divergent Thinking', Avner Ziv, *Contemporary Educational Psychology*; Vol. 8, No. 1, pp. 68–75, January 1983.

> This is another example of what I call 'breaking the plane' (see my story about Bob Dylan in Chapter 6).
>
> One time the film director Paul Verhoeven[8] was getting frustrated and angry in the recording studio and no-one could understand why he was so upset. I was looking on incredulously while people like my brilliant and trusted engineer and film music producer Steve McClaughlin were saying they were quitting. At the same time, to add to the tension, there was a 60-piece orchestra sitting waiting to play the next piece of music. I went out of the studio, put on a woman's dress and earrings, burst back into the studio and insisted on dancing with Paul. At first he was in shock, then he started laughing and so did everyone else and the session got going again.

THE JOKER

Throwing something into the mix to add freshness to thinking is always a good idea.

Theatre and film director Matthew Warchus told Business Playground how a single word in a new way can give a scene a whole new meaning: 'I was working on Shakespeare's *Much Ado About Nothing* right in the beginning of my career in my early 20s. There's a speech in it where one the characters talks about the 'career of his affections', and it was being acted as though the actor meant developing progress of his affections from bachelor to married man – sort of growing up – but I looked up the word during rehearsals and found that the word 'career' had one meaning at the time the play was written, and that was 'sharp and sudden changes of direction'.

[8]Paul Verhoeven's directing credits include *RoboCop* (1987), *Total Recall* (1990), *Basic Instinct* (1992), *Starship Troopers* (1997) and *Hollow Man* (2000).

We still sometimes use it. We see a horse and cart careering across the road, or a vehicle careering out of control. I thought that was really useful because we've somehow taken that word and made it a really ordinary word like 'plan' or 'progress of logical steps from A to B to C to D'. But it's the opposite: sharp and sudden unexpected changes of direction. And I think that's really helpful. In life people are able to think about their careers or their work or the way that they think or whatever it is like that.'[9]

The banana-skin technique uses an outrageous joke or visual to help people to creatively change their direction. Here's a technique that does it by adding in a random element to spark some ideas using a set of 'Joker' cards to pick from when a little push is needed. On each card is a suggestion for where to find inspiration; just throw a dice to choose which one.

Look in the fridge. Pick up a couple of items and for each one look at the packaging, the design, the ingredients and any instructions. Think about when you last used it and when you're planning to use it next. What does it make you feel? What's good about it? What's bad? How can you relate it to the creative problem you're working on?

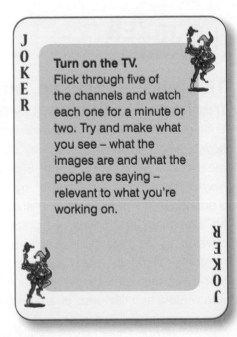

Turn on the TV. Flick through five of the channels and watch each one for a minute or two. Try and make what you see – what the images are and what the people are saying – relevant to what you're working on.

[9]When he heard this, Dave realised for the first time he does actually have a 'career'.

JOKER **JOKER**

Open up a newspaper. Quickly pick two or three articles, without thinking too much about which ones, and read the first few paragraphs. Think about the stories and the people involved. Think about what your story should be and how the stories you're reading connect to it.

JOKER **JOKER**

Browse through a magazine. Look at the ads and pictures. Why do they look the way they do? What are they trying to convey about the advertisers or its products? How significant is the style, the layout and the colours? What ideas do they spark about your own project?

JOKER **JOKER**

Go to 'Stumble Upon' on the web. Stumble Upon (www.stumbleupon.com) is a great way to randomly discover websites that you might otherwise never find. You enter in the areas that interest you then hit 'stumble' and it'll take you to a randomly generated web page. Do this five or six times and you will stumble upon something you'll realise is relevant to your project. Guaranteed.

JOKER **JOKER**

Go to the library or bookshop. Randomly pick out three books from different sections that you wouldn't normally look at. Take them to a seating area and spend 10 or 15 minutes with each, flicking through them and stopping to read passages that catch your eye. Take time to read about the author, think about what made him or her want to write the book in the first place and try to picture what their lives are like. Think about how they'd approach your own project. What would the title of the book be?

When Annie and I had our first hits, instead of recording in a straightforward expensive recording studio in London or New York I would come up with crazy places to set up equipment and start making an album. These odd locations triggered different moods and helped keep our records sounding unusual and fresh.

The album *Be Yourself Tonight*, an album that included the number-one hit song *There Must Be An Angel Playing With My Heart* (with Stevie Wonder on harmonica) and other hits like *Would I Lie to You* and *Sisters Are Doing It For Themselves* (a duet with Aretha Franklin), was mostly recorded in a small room in a youth club in the suburbs of Paris! The French teenagers hanging around the club didn't believe we were making an album until the BBC turned up to interview us for a TV show. So there we were, very famous at the time and could have been recording in luxury anywhere in the world; instead we made our way to the outskirts of Paris every day and up lots of stairs fighting our way through table-tennis matches and tip-toeing through ballet lessons into a tiny room that Annie decorated from the flea market, to start the day's recording experiments.

On the album *We Too Are One* we hired a suite in a legendary rock and roll hotel called the Mayflower overlooking Central Park (not as glamorous as you might think, it was at the time a very run-down hotel with lots of cockroaches). We set up our recording gear and started making an album in the hotel suite, every now and then going for walks down 8th Avenue or in Central Park and then back in the elevator up to our suite to record Annie's vocal or me playing a guitar track. Being in the hotel is a completely different thing from being in a sterile studio environment, and there are lots of things there to stimulate you – like the bar, for instance!

(It was the same bar years ago where I first met Madonna and, even though she was just starting her career, I could tell she had her head screwed on. And boy does she know how to play in the Business Playground!)

CHAOS THEORY

If creativity is about making connections between two seemingly unconnected things, then another way to throw something random into the mix is to use arbitrary words. Try this: grab a dictionary and randomly pick out a word then force a connection between it and the problem you're trying to solve. We did it to see what would happen with the *traffic congestion in LA* problem. The word we randomly picked by speedily flicking through the pages and then plopping an ink-stained finger on a page was: 'donation'. Then we thought, 'Um, that's a hard one, maybe we should try again and pretend we hadn't found that one,' but then honesty kicked in. We realised if we did that it wouldn't be random, it would in fact be *cheating*, so decided to go with it and force ourselves to quickly come up with solutions for the traffic congestion in LA problem that, somehow or other, relate to the idea of donation.

After a couple of minutes of pondering this what we came up with:

- Drivers could be made to donate to charity every time they drive.
- People could be asked to donate their cars to charity and use other means of transport.
- There could be a donation drive to build a better form of transport.
- Companies could be encouraged to sponsor free bus passes to donate to commuters.
- Employers could be asked to donate one day a week of their employees' time to work that doesn't require them to travel.

Not that any of these are amazing ideas, but what struck us about the process was this: *it actually works.* **Yes folks, if you get past that initial barrier of thinking there's no obvious connection between your problem and the word you've randomly picked, you can force yourself to come up with ideas, some of which might be worth pursuing.** The other thing that struck us (and might have struck you too) was that in retrospect the word we randomly picked *might not have been that random after all.* Maybe subconsciously we picked 'donation' by filtering out some of the other words on that page ('donkey', 'door', 'doodle', 'dong', 'doom', to name a few) that we thought would be non-starters. It's possible, but then again maybe it doesn't really matter that the subconscious mind rather than the conscious one made the choice (see Chapter 5). The point of the exercise is to introduce stimuli that seem unrelated to the problem we're trying to solve and, even if the subconscious is pushing us in a certain direction, perhaps that's just fine.

Incidentally, we have created a game called *SLAP!* as a fun way for making connections between random words. It is in the form of a pack of playing cards so we couldn't include it in the book, but here's a sample and you can find out more at **www.businessplayground.com**

Instructions

1. There are four suits of 15 cards each showing a different word.
2. Divide the 52 cards equally amongst the players.
3. Players take turns putting cards face up on a pile in the middle, looking for two with the same face value.
4. The first player who sees two that match and shouts 'SLAP!' has 60 seconds to come up with a single word that connects the two words on the cards (a possible answer to the one shown is 'caterpillar').
5. If the player comes up with a word in time he or she picks up all the cards in the pile.
6. The winner is the first to collect all of the cards.

Sometimes writers get what they call 'writers block'. It's traumatising and a vortex, as the more they worry the worse it gets. I've often helped snap them out of it by being either very humorous, crazy or taking them on an adventure. I've done this with everyone from Bryan Ferry to Katy Perry and I'm sure a few other people rhyming in 'erry'. Sometimes getting blind drunk helps. Or the opposite – a great picnic in the countryside with a traditional picnic basket and all the right accoutrements. Involving them in the shopping for cheese, garlic sausage, etc., takes their mind off the problem with the lyrics and it's great for me because I love picnics.[10]

Of course, one of the things about good ideas is that often they seem very obvious afterwards and so we are prone to discount the thinking that went into creating them. Paul Allen, co-founder of Microsoft, told Business Playground, 'To me it's like a moment of obviousness. While there's an obvious idea here: take a simple programming language and connect it with a microprocessor, maybe that's a really great idea. It seems so obvious and then you go, "Wait a minute, has anybody else figured it out, or are they on the same track?" And if they're not you really have to follow up and jump on the idea and see if you can make it happen and a lot of times it means forming a team of people, or of course in your case a rock band, around a certain musical style, and then it's a lot of hard work to make it real, to actualise it.'

[10]Brian Eno and Peter Schmidt came out with some playing cards called *Oblique Strategies* that have cryptic remarks on them and can help break a deadlock or solve a dilemma.

In fact, one entrepreneur has built his whole business around the notion that in retrospect good ideas are obvious. Evan Williams is co-founder and CEO of Twitter, the social networking platform that made it big in 2008, and the company he created to develop Twitter was initially called Obvious for that very reason. **Twitter might seem like an obvious idea now – give friends a way to tell one another what they're up to – but on paper it really wasn't.** Doing is believing and when you've done it you know why it works, but trying to explain why it works to someone who hasn't tried it is difficult, to say the least. We mean, why you would develop another form of keeping in touch when you've already got your online profile, blogs, email, phone, IM, not to mention plain old meeting face-to-face (known as F2F in the online world)?

Evan told us that he didn't even try to convince investors of the value of Twitter before it was a real product. 'It would have been a tough sell,' he says. He and his team of developers built a prototype of Twitter along with some other applications they'd been working on to try them out. 'Once we had the prototype and were using it ourselves, then it was very clear it was interesting. It was immediately compelling to the small group of us using it.' Even when they launched Twitter it didn't take off right away and Evan eventually bought the company back from the original investors, but by 2008 it was a runaway success with a valuation in the many millions.[11]

[11]The reported valuation of Twitter had reached $1 billion by September 2009.

Twitter's use has gradually changed over time from giving friends trivial updates, or 'Tweets', in answer to the question 'What are you doing?' to being a way for people to keep in touch with what's happening on a much broader scale. No longer just learning that your pal Joe is having a cup of joe,[12] but also updates on politics, favourite bands and sports teams or whatever else you decide to sign up to. 'It's continually surprising,' Evan says. 'Even though we have had the notion for a while that Twitter has the potential to be very big, it's the way it's grown and the different uses and the reality of it becoming big in so many different ways that is always surprising.' Obvious, right?

ON THE CONTRARY

If you think about it, most problems are contradictions between two opposing factors. An umbrella needs to be small and unobtrusive when it's dry, big and strong when it's raining. How can something that needs to be folded up into a small package that can stuffed in a bag also be unfolded into a large canopy that won't break or blow away when it's windy? **Taking time to understand the contradictions inherent within a problem often helps us to find innovative solutions to solve it.** Take the electric car, for instance. As you might know they've been around in one form or another for decades. The first one was developed by Thomas Davenport of New Hampshire in 1834. His ran on rails using a battery for power that couldn't be recharged. Later that century, after the rechargeable battery had been invented, electric cars became popular in Europe and then in the US as smoother and quieter alternatives to cars powered by

[12] Or, coffee.

internal combustion engines. By 1897 the Electric Carriage and Wagon Company of Philadelphia had built a fleet of electric-powered New York taxis, and at one point, just before the turn of the century, electric cars even outsold petrol-powered ones.

But that was then and this is now. Since, electric cars have almost disappeared because of an inherent contradiction between two factors: the weight of the battery and the performance of the car. To make longer trips than just local journeys, especially getting up any reasonable speed, requires a great big battery. And the car has to carry that heavy battery around, so using up a lot of power. The electric car just doesn't make sense for long journeys. **One innovator has realised there might be a way to remove the contradiction if a network of battery recharging centres could be created that were close enough to one another, so a small battery would be sufficient for each section of the journey.** Shai Agassi is the founder of A Better Place, a company based in Paolo Alto, California, that aims to build a personable and scalable public transportation that ends our dependence on oil (in other words, *a better place*). Working with governments, regions and cities, A Better Place is building a network of recharging spots and battery replacement stations. And when people aren't using their electric car, say while they're at home or at work, they can plug it in to top up the battery charge. For longer journeys there will be places along the route where you can change batteries for a fully recharged one without leaving the car and in less time than it takes to full up a tank with petrol.

The whole system is completely automated. The charge spots are the size of parking meters, and when a driver pulls up to one of them a computer on board the car tells it to link up to the charger and start charging the battery. At battery-replacement stations a driver simply pulls up and sits back, and within three minutes a new fully-charged battery has replaced the depleted one. Drivers will pay a subscription charge to use the system, much like they do for their mobile phones, but instead of buying minutes they'll be buying miles. A Better Place has already signed up Israel, Canada, Australia, Denmark, Hawaii and Bay Area cities in California to participate in the scheme and Renault is already building electric cars for it.

Agassi's idea shows the power of bringing together two opposing forces. Just like a banana skin and a shoe. But how about going on step further, and forgetting batteries altogether? Instead, powering electric vehicles directly from the grid, South Korea is experimenting with cars that pull in power from cables beneath the road. According to the developer of the project, Korea's Advanced Institute of Science and Technology (KAIST), power from two nuclear systems would be enough to run six million cars. **Sounds to us like one big fun Scalextric set!**

MOVE ONE SPACE FORWARD TO THE NEXT CHAPTER ... OR ROLL THE DICE

Being in control is very reassuring in business situations, while chaos goes against the grain. However, once in a while we need to impose a little orchestrated chaos to get the creative engines revving. **Great writers and musicians throughout the ages have used techniques involving randomness to create amazing work, and in business we can learn from that.** Humour is one way of introducing an unexpected element into the mix and to change the direction of thinking that might be getting stale as old bread, and it has been shown to have a direct relationship to creative ability. Creativity is about connecting two seemingly unconnected, often opposing pieces, and as Paul Allen and Evan Williams have shown, the resulting idea often in retrospect seems obvious. So now that we've tried a bunch of techniques to come up with some new ideas, in the next chapter we decide which ones to move forward with, and which ones to say a sad farewell to.

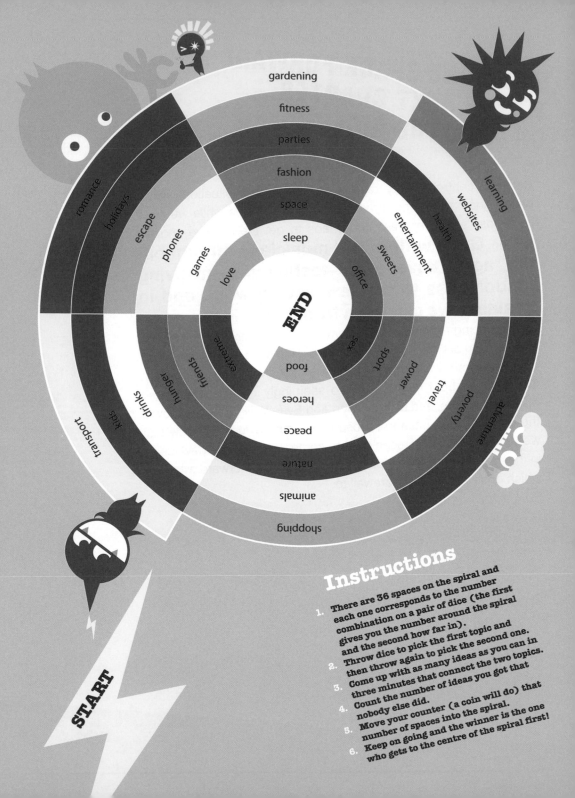

gardening
fitness
parties
fashion
space
sleep

romance
holidays
escape
phones
games
love

learning
websites
health
entertainment
sweets
office

transport
kids
drinks
hunger
friends
extreme

adventure
poverty
travel
power
sport
sex

shopping
animals
nature
peace
heroes
food

END

START

Instructions

1. There are 36 spaces on the spiral and each one corresponds to the number combination on a pair of dice (the first gives you the number around the spiral and the second how far in).

2. Throw dice to pick the first topic and then throw again to pick the second one.

3. Come up with as many ideas as you can in three minutes that connect the two topics.

4. Count the number of ideas you got that nobody else did.

5. Move your counter (a coin will do) that number of spaces into the spiral.

6. Keep on going and the winner is the one who gets to the centre of the spiral first!

BOARD GAME: INSPIRAL

How it works: Making connections between seemingly unrelated things is at the very heart of creativity and this game *forces* us to make those connections to come up with something entirely new!

How to play: A player roles two dice to find the first theme, then rolls them again to find the second. The number combinations of the dice identify which space to go to (e.g. throwing a 4 and a 3 on the first roll means go to the space that is 4 around the spiral and 3 in towards the centre), and so which theme. Now players have three minutes to come up with as many ideas, sensible or crazy, as they can think of that link the two themes.

After every turn players count up the number of ideas they each came up with that are unique (meaning, distinct from one another), and move their counters to the corresponding number of spaces around the spiral of the board, moving inwards towards the centre of the spiral. So, if a player came up with three unique ideas then he or she moves three spaces around the board towards its centre.

Example: The first theme might be 'sweets' and the second theme 'animals', and so players need to think of ideas that link the two – such as sweets shaped like animals, or sweets to give to animals as treats. Or maybe sweets made from chicken to give to children as a way to sneak protein into their diets. (We know, calm down … it's just an example.)

To win: The first player to reach the centre of the spiral is the winner.

CHAPTER ELEVEN
KILL THE IDEA

Choosing which ideas to focus our time, money and energy on.

There are some pretty terrible ideas out there that have somehow made it to the shelves, shopping channels and, pretty quickly afterwards, dustbins. Take, for example, the facial exerciser, a small spring device that looks like a deformed rodent skeleton you're supposed to wedge into either side of your mouth and flex to work the muscles of the chin, neck and face. Apparently it gives users a more youthful appearance without the need for surgery and is 'clinically proven' to be safe and effective. It also makes the user look like The Joker from *Batman*. Surely this is an idea that should have been strangled at birth? Or take the pocket fishing rod. No, this is not a euphemism for something else – it really is a pocket fishing rod. It features a telescopic rod to allow you to fish whenever the mood strikes and some of the more intriguing models also double as a pen. Included in the kit are a hook, line and sinker. That's right … hook, line and sinker.

How do we know which of our own ideas are worth keeping and which are not?

If we've being playing hard enough, and flexed our creative muscles,[1] we should by now have a ton of possibilities. But we have to whittle these down to, first, a shortlist of the strongest contenders, and then ultimately a single idea that we are prepared to focus our energies on and do whatever it takes to bring to life (although, with practice, you might be able to keep a few ideas going at once – see page 192). In the idea creation phase we tried not to be too hampered by practicalities, but now a healthy dose of reality needs to come into play. This is the territory of the left side of our brains. In the playing part of the innovation process, in which we generated the pool of ideas, the right halves were in command and the sensible left halves had to wait it out on the sidelines, but now it's their turn.

[1] As opposed to our facial muscles.

IT'S A GAME OF TWO HALVES

The left would have been warming up, jogging on the spot and doing stretching exercises while the more zany other half was on the field in the thick of things. Now the coach (we're not sure where this metaphor's going, but we'll carry on a couple more sentences just to see) beckons to the left side to take off its tracksuit and come on to the field. The right half looks a bit dejected at first, but has had a good game and knows its energy reserves are low. It's time for some fresh blood. The two hemispheres tap hands as they pass one another, passing the metaphorical baton (a metaphor within a metaphor – now this is getting crazy), signalling 'well done' from the left and 'good luck' from the right. Right goes to the bench to get its breath back and recover. Left is already on the field running hard, getting stuck in. We could go on, but we won't.

Left brain's skill is analysing the ideas to see which ones are practical and have a chance of succeeding and it has a few tricks up its sleeve to help. **The simplest method is to categorise the ideas as ones that are feasible now, those that have potential and ones that are just too weird. But even with these weirdos it's important not to discard them outright, however oddball.** They should be noted down for future reference, maybe for another project, while the ideas that seem feasible right now and those that have potential can be worked on a little further (... the right half of the brain looks up hopefully from the bench realising he might be called on to play a bit more). To get ourselves into the frame of mind of considering how any of the more feasible ideas might be implemented, a handy technique is to start by writing it up as: 'What I see myself doing is ...'. Then jot down things we think are great about our idea, potential spin-offs from it, and practical concerns that we have about it.

So, for example …

Finding companies to sponsor kitted-out minibuses as an alternative form of transportation to people driving to and from work.

This is great because …	People can leave their cars at home so reduce their greenhouse gas emissions.	They can do work on the way so can spend less time in the office.	They can connect with new people and swap ideas.
It could also lead to …	Additional revenue streams through corporate sponsorships and from selling coffee and snacks on board the bus.	People can get rid of one of their cars and use the money to pay for a holiday for the family.	As on a school bus, there will be a feeling of community spirit with commuters getting to know people in their neighbourhoods.
It worries me that …	The logistics of finding good pick-up and drop-off points will make the service difficult to operate.	Everyone starts and finishes work at different times so there'd have to be multiple services throughout the day.	People are so wedded to driving their own cars it'll take a huge change in attitude to make it work.

Doing an exercise like this one will do more than help us edit down the ideas to the strongest few, it will also enable us to improve upon those suckers. We can begin to think through how we'd build enthusiasm for the idea, what resources we'd need to implement it and maybe how we'd test it. We should ask ourselves what other stakeholders would think about the ideas. We might want to do a role-playing exercise to help think about who are key stakeholders that will have an influence on whether the idea is likely to happen. Stakeholders could be a local official, for instance, or a consumer advocate group, a regulatory body, a venture capitalist, a bank, a finance director, a CEO, your husband, wife, the dog, etc. In all likelihood there'll be a bunch of them who can make or break what we're trying to do, the movers and shakers who can make the difference between the idea failing or, hopefully, succeeding.

Now put yourself into their shoes (see Chapter 9, Shoe Swapper). For each one of the stakeholders ask yourself: *What's in it for them? Why would they be interested in helping you do this, or at least not stand in your way? What is it about the idea that they'll see as a negative? Does it conflict with other things they are trying to do? Will it make their life more difficult in any respect?* Unfortunately it's far easier for people to say 'no' to new ideas and to leave things as they are rather than change things (see the section on naysayers in Chapter 1), however much sense change would seem to make – at least to us innovators. Empathising with the key stakeholders can help us understand how they'll look at our ideas and allows us to find ways to eradicate any problems before they are ever even exposed to them. We're not talking 'eradicate' as in 'wipe out' Mafia-style, but after all other avenues have been explored, do consider good old bribes and blackmail as a last resort.[2]

[2]We're joking.

People shouldn't be afraid of having many ideas going at the same time. You have an idea, and that might spark another idea, but you don't drop the first idea to do the new one, you keep it spinning like a plate and then you go to the other idea. And the new one might make you think of yet another idea, so now you have three or four. They might all be connected a little bit but they've become their own thing, and then you notice this idea – the fifth one along – is going much faster than the other ones, so you say, that's OK, I'll follow this fifth one but I'll keep the others just spinning along. And then when you see one going really, really wonky and about to fall off you look at it and maybe think, well that's alright, I've got these 32 other ideas and they're going just fine.

What I find is wandering between the different ideas and projects is very inspirational because I haven't been obsessed with the same thing for three months, so I can come in completely fresh to each one. At the end of the time I feel quite worn out but happy that I haven't been stuck in the same problem over and over again. In many businesses they have one thing that they do; there's always got to be at least one person in the company who is not satisfied with the way things are right now. It's interesting to be constantly looking at your business as an ever-evolving thing. If you don't do that in this day and age, where everything changes every 24 hours, you'll be dead.

CAN YOU FEEL IT?

Picking out the one great idea from the pool of good ones you've been working on is not always easy. First, it's difficult to be objective. You've been so involved in creating them that you might find it hard to separate the wheat from the chaff, the men from the boys, the pandas from the squirrels. Second, you're now emotionally invested in the ideas. If they've made it this far, there's something about them you like and it's difficult to let go. But, let go you must, even if it takes cold hard cash. Merck, the research and pharmaceutical giant, has developed a system to kill ideas it's working on if they look like they're not going anywhere. They offer 'kill fees', by handing out options as a reward to scientists who bail out on losing projects.[3] They are rewarding the decision to move on. Merck research and development chief Peter Kim said of the scheme, 'You can't change the truth. You can only delay how long it takes to find it out.'[4]

Getting feedback from others, whether consumers or colleagues or lovers, is one way to decide on the one winner. They are more likely to be objective than you. But, buyer beware, we can't rely too heavily on the opinions of others. Their judgement will be only as good as the materials they're given to judge, and in many cases we can't adequately communicate our idea without actually going and doing it. We'll come back to that. Meanwhile, let's not ignore the power of gut. **Even if we can't always put into words why we think one idea is better than another, for some reason the right one often just feels right.**

[3]'Creativity and the Role of the Leader', Teresa M. Amabile and Mukti Khaire, *Harvard Business Review*, October 2008.

[4]'Is Merck Medicine Working?', *Business Week*, 30 July 2007.

Freddie DeMann, a veteran music producer, has an amazing career spanning over three decades and has managed both Michael Jackson and Madonna. 'You know, I'd like to say there's a little bit of an artist in me,' he told Business Playground. 'When I was a kid I took drum lessons and I took tap dance and when I was about 20 I took acting lessons. I thought I wanted to be an artist, but was wise enough to realise I didn't have "the stuff". I'm not in this business by accident, I'm in this business called show business, but it's the arts that I like and being close to artists and I like being close to the creative process. It's what gets my rocks off. It's what gets me up every morning with enthusiasm. When I was a manager I told people I was the bridge between art and commerce. And thank God I have a pretty good business mind. But I always have an artistic mind and I think that gives me some special credentials, and I love what I do so much. God gave me a good ear to recognise a hit song and, by extension, a hit song is a hit script, is a book, is a play, is a show.'

He told Business Playground about how gut instinct has helped him recognise potential hits. **'You just know it,' he said. 'It's like when somebody plays a song for you and you hear eight bars and you know it's a smash.'** Often the artists themselves don't know which of their work is just good and which is so great that it will take the charts by storm. 'It takes someone else to say *this*, this is the smash, and not this.' He gives an example: 'I've had a lot of experience with that. I was managing The Jacksons way back in 1978 and at that time they had left Motown and gone to Epic and they weren't hot, they were kind of cold, they were ice cold, and they were also in disarray and they were fighting amongst themselves. I told them there's one hit on this album and *that's* what we're putting out. It's called *Shake Your Body Down To The Ground*. I was right, it sold two million singles and caused the album to go platinum[5] and that was the rebirth of

[5]In fact it made double-platinum status from the Recording Industry Association of America.

The Jacksons, which led to Quincy Jones producing Michael and having those two incredible albums, *Off The Wall* and *Thriller*.'

We asked Freddie if he had a process or technique for recognising the winning ideas, the ones that would be hits. He said, 'I hate to disappoint you, but I don't know the answer to that. Very often I have myriad thoughts that are kind of rushing through and it's very distracting. But if something is really, really good and it grabs you by the throat, those thoughts stay away and you're completely engulfed in what you're hearing.' He adds, 'When you were playing *Hole in the Fence*,[6] I was already thinking what theatre it should open in New York. I was already thinking who I'm going to get on the production team, who should be augmenting what you've done. So, yes, I do tend to race ahead when I'm enthusiastic about something.'

The role of gut instinct in picking the winner is confirmed by Evan Williams, co-founder and CEO of online social networking tool Twitter.
Prior to launching Twitter, Evan had launched a blog publishing system called Blogger, which his team had developed as a by-product to another project. Evan told Business Playground, 'It wasn't at all what our company was planning to do, it was very much just an idea on the side which seemed like a very small idea compared to what we were working on.' But, he says, 'I just couldn't get rid of the Blogger idea, it kept nagging me.' Evan and his team pursued with Blogger and it eventually became a huge success.[7]

Christian Audigier, creative genius behind clothing labels Von Dutch and Ed Hardy, describes 'just knowing' when an idea has the potential to be big. In 2000 he was brought in as the head designer for Von Dutch. The clothing label is named after car and motorbike 'pinstriper'[8] Kenneth Graeme Howar, who had often signed his work

[6]The title song Dave wrote for a stage musical.

[7]They sold their company, Pyra, to Google in 2003.

[8]Pinstriping is the application of very thin lines of paint.

'Von Dutch'. 'Von Dutch was the Pope of the pinstripe,' Christian told Business Playground. **He wanted to create a lifestyle brand that conjured up images of garages, custom cars and bikes. 'It would make you feel like someone else,' he says.** Despite having no formal training in branding or marketing, Christian has a great instinct for what will work and as soon as he saw the iconic Von Dutch signature he thought, 'If I do that big I'm going to be the new Abercrombie and Fitch.' His initial idea was to put the name on T-shirts and to give them to celebrities, but in a remarkable use of 'the answer is in the question' (see Chapter 4), Christian looked from the other end of the telescope and thought, if a celebrity is going to be all over magazines and newspapers, it's usually their head and shoulders that will be guaranteed to be in the picture so, boom, he decided to use trucker hats instead, with plenty of room to have Von Dutch sprawled across their high fronts!

He managed to persuade Britney Spears when at the peak of her fame to wear Von Dutch clothing, although it wasn't easy. 'In the beginning when you try to see Britney Spears you are a stupid 45-year old man talking to a 16-year-old girl and you don't even know any of her songs,' he says. But he managed to convince her and then boyfriend Justin Timberlake. A week later the couple split up and pictures of them were splashed across the cover of *People* magazine, both wearing Von Dutch trucker caps. The brand took off overnight and the craze for trucker caps was born. Christian left Von Dutch a little while later to start his own clothing line, Ed Hardy (it sounds like 'Edardee' when Christian says it in his strong French accent), a high-end clothing line inspired by the work of American tattoo artist Don Ed Hardy ('the godfather of tattoo'). Christian wanted to make it into a lifestyle brand with the vibe of being in a gang and, again, his gut instinct told him this was a winning idea. He now sells the line in retailers around the world including a string of Ed Hardy shops in major cities, has over 200 licensees, and sales are approaching a billion dollars a year.

So now you have a plate full of ideas, a knife and fork and a fresh pot of coffee. Which ideas look the most appetising and which ones just look like a mess of spaghetti? Or, if you have no clue, dig in and see which one hangs on to your fork! It's fairly easy to dig away and spot the no-hopers and throw them in the trash, but when it gets down to the last pieces of linguini you may have three or four that stick right on that plate or twist around your fork and it's very difficult to then just choose the one to play with.

What I do is write down two or three words on each idea like: 'fit 'n' green'. This idea is about turning fitness centres into generators that give the members rewards based on the amount of electricity they generate. This would lead to home applications on fitness bikes and a brand that can make anything from fitness games to walking phone chargers, etc. I don't need to write all the stuff describing it, I just write 'fit 'n' green' and if I can't remember what it's all about in a week's time then it can't have been that good, so I kill it.

It's exactly the same as songwriting. If you can't remember the melody that you wrote a week earlier, then it's not a good one. Sometimes when I give talks to big companies I get them to compose a song on the spot about their company mission. It's good fun having the whole company trying to explain what they are about by writing a song or a chorus. It forces them to break the whole thing down into a few words and a hook (meaning a catchy melody). During the talk I record it and at the end of the session play it back sounding like a finished record, and 24 hours later it has often been posted up on their website!

Killing ideas is very painful and sometimes they come back to haunt you. You think fit 'n' green is dead in the water then you walk past a new gym on your way back from Starbucks and you see lots of women in leotards through the window peddling furiously alongside a few heavyweight middle-aged men fast-walking, frantically clutching on to the side rails. You look up and see it's called 'The Powerhouse' and it says that it's the first green-energy producing gym franchise, and you choke on your doughnut.

Ideas come back to haunt you in other ways. You thought you killed the idea about the cartoon character called Mr Macaroni and Noodles (his dog), but in the middle of the night you wake up singing his theme song and can't help seeing him happy as Larry in his junkyard on Nickelodeon![9] This is when it becomes impossible to kill the idea but it keeps popping up in your head wherever you look. You are at dinner and you look over your vodka martini and you see the maître d' and he looks very like Mr Macaroni. By your second martini you are scribbling Macaroni notes on the tablecloth and offering to pay for damages.

So in the end I had to let Mr Macaroni live and I put him back in the spaghetti bowl. Now Paul Pethick, a brilliant animator and writer, and I have partnered on it and we have a wonderful animated presentation, as well as booklets and Macaroni inventions of old musical shoes and other products based on Mr Macaroni and his pooch. In fact, it became an idea chosen by Nickelodeon to be developed, along with two other ideas, as a series they might potentially launch. Alas, they mistakenly chose Mr Meaty[10] over our brilliant work, but Macaroni still lives on and, because this idea has survived both my attempt at murder and the cruel treatment of Nickelodeon, he and Noodles are well prepared for survival. They are now just playing around the junkyard, biding their time, waiting to see if we are part of a bouquet of kids' shows in a subscription world on mobile phones or whether we will just 'Club Penguin'[11] them into superstardom!

[9]Nickelodeon is a TV network aimed at kids and owned by Viacom.

[10]Oddly-shaped puppets working at the fast-food *Mr Meaty* restaurant.

[11]**www.clubpenguin.com** is a very successful online virtual world for kids that's raking in the fish … er, we mean cash.

MOVE ONE SPACE FORWARD TO THE NEXT CHAPTER ... OR ROLL THE DICE

Once we've created a bunch of ideas using the techniques we've outlined in the book, we need to find out which ones are worth focusing serious time, effort and resources on, and which should be killed off. Some companies, recognising the need to move on from ideas that don't have enough potential, will actually pay their scientists to kill them. This next stage is where the analytical left half of the brain takes over from the more creative right half. A sort of exercise that will help determine which ones are feasible and what we could do to improve them and make them work. **As Freddie DeMann, Evan Williams and Christian Audigier explained, when all is said and done gut instinct plays a big role in deciding whether an idea is a BIG idea.** As for the crazy ideas that we can't find a place for now, they should be put aside; but we should not lose them as sometimes they will come back to haunt us. Now, in the last chapter let's add some rocket fuel and find out what it takes in an organisation to put ideas into orbit!

18
10
1
3
6
19
13
5
4
17
11
2
8
15
16
12
7
9
14
7

Instructions

1. When you have a bunch of ideas to choose from, pick 19 and number them.
2. Now close your eyes and randomly plop a finger down on the board. Kill the idea that you pick ... or give it one of the three lives you have.
3. The three lives can only be used on two different ideas.
4. The winning idea is the one on which you've used two of the three lives. All the others die.

BOARD GAME: KILL THE IDEA

How it works: Sometimes we instinctively know when an idea is worth keeping and when another isn't, but we need a little push to make that difficult choice. Being made to choose helps us realise which one of them really matters.

How to play: Write down 19 of the strongest ideas for the problem you are trying to solve and number them 1–19. Now close your eyes and plonk a finger randomly down on to the board. The number it lands on determines which one of the ideas will be killed. But, don't despair quite yet, you have three 'saves' to give an idea that has been killed the chance to live again. By forcing yourself to murder your ideas, but with a chance to give them a stay of execution, you'll soon realise which one feels like the one idea worth fighting for.

The three saves can be used on only two different ideas, and so the winning idea is the one on which two of the three saves have been used. For example, say you are working on ideas for getting publicity for your new venture and included in the 19 ideas you've shortlisted are: get the CEO to 'do a Branson' and appear in public just in his underpants; donate time and services to people who need help in the community and tell the local paper; or get a celebrity to use one of your products and hope they'll be photographed doing so. If having plonked a finger on the Branson idea as one to kill you might decide it's worth saving and so use a life. But, then only two lives are left. Then the community work idea comes up – is it worth saving or not, knowing that if you do save it, because the saves can only be used on two different ideas, you cannot save any of the others? You decide, nah, it isn't worth saving – kill it! The needy can fend for themselves. After a few more finger plonks on the board and some more deaths (we're talking about the ideas we've killed here, not the needy) the celebrity photo op idea comes up and you decide this one is worth saving. Two lives used up and one to go, and now it's decision time. The only two ideas left in the running are the ones you've saved (which is why you always have to choose the two ideas you use those two lives on very carefully) and it's going to be sudden death between them. Toss a coin to find out which must die, and use your last life if your gut tells you that the one that comes up is the one idea you cannot live without.

CHAPTER TWELVE
BLAST OFF!

Creating environments that put creativity into orbit.

'Vision without action is hallucination.' Benjamin Franklin

Following through with ideas is as important as having them in the first place so they don't just become conversation fodder for cocktail parties ('I had this great idea once. You should have seen the size of it. Huh … wonder whatever happened to it …?'). Most great ideas only saw the light of day as a result of the tireless perseverance of an individual or group of dedicated people, each of whom had battled against all odds. In fact, it takes blood, sweat and tears (and luckily there are washing powders that will get rid of even the toughest of stains). Inventor James Dyson built 5,127 prototypes of his bagless vacuum cleaner, the Dual Cyclone, before he perfected his design, yet all the major vacuum cleaner manufacturers who were making too much money selling vacuum cleaner bags rejected it. Hoover Vice-President, Mike Rutter, later said on national television, 'I do regret that Hoover as a company did not take the product technology off Dyson; it would have lain on the shelf and not been used.'[1]

Having conviction in the idea is vital. Even if it's not perfect yet, belief in it will have an effect on others who might realise it's an unstoppable train that they should get on, or miss and lose out on a big opportunity. Sometimes you just need to take a deep breath, look supremely confident, and go for it. Henry Ford said, 'If you think you can, or if you think you can't, you're right.' Burt Rutan, who ran the team that developed the Voyager spacecraft, said, 'Confidence in nonsense is required.'[2] And it's said by people who have worked with Apple co-founder Steve Jobs that he has a

[1]'www.telegraph.co.uk/finance/newsbysector/supportservices/2795244/James-Dyson-the-vacuum-dreamer.html

[2]'The Weird Rules of Creativity', Robert Sutton, *Harvard Business Review*, September 2001.

'reality distortion field', or a spell that he casts on those around him, convincing them of the success of an idea. Not that any of what Steve Jobs does is nonsense; it's just that he just has an amazing knack for selling the ideas he likes.

Christian Audigier, who runs his own billion-dollar clothing empire, says in his wonderful French accent that, 'You need to insist to exist. If you don't insist, you're not going to exist.

Someone can close a door – this one doesn't want you – you can come back a week later or a month later and one day this door's going to open for you, you know.' His success with Von Dutch gave him his moment in the spotlight, his 15 minutes of fame, but he still had to work incredibly hard to make inroads with his own venture,[3] Ed Hardy. He had to prove to the retailers that he could deliver. To launch the brand to them he put on his own trade show in Las Vegas that competed head-on with MAGIC, traditionally the largest gathering of men's fashion-buyers in the US. His show was called *When I Move, You Move*. It was an expensive and audacious ploy that got the attention of the whole fashion industry – something that just having a booth at MAGIC would never have done. The next year the organisers of MAGIC came to Christian asking him to collaborate with them. He moved and they moved.

In addition to Ed Hardy, Christian Audigier is developing other fashion projects that break the mould, including the high-end casualwear label Crystal Rock with his daughter and, with Dave, Rock Fabulous, a rock-and-roll lifestyle brand. When Business Playground interviewed Christian he had recently been in conversations with Madonna about creating a whole fashion empire around the Madonna brand.

---

[3]He was head designer at Von Dutch, but it was owned by Tonny Sorensen.

'Today I'm working on a potential new project with Madonna,' he said. 'Her management told me she wants to build an empire, and I thought "That's great"; she has huge assets, she has her name, her song titles, her album titles, she has a lot of pictures of herself, she has reinvented herself every two years – spiritual Kabala woman, material girl, erotica girl. So what I proposed was we do something that involved the three tiers of the fashion business – Neiman Marcus, Bloomingdales and Target[4] – so she can be merchandised everywhere. The idea is to separate out her life story. One brand would be *Erotica*, that's going to be for the upper tiers like Neiman Marcus. We would have *True Blue*, the title of one of her albums, in Bloomingdales, and we'd have the *Like A Virgin* brand for Target. And I believe we can go to all those tiers at the same time.'

Christian's philosophy is that iconic artists such as Madonna, the Stones, Kanye West, or even actors like Jack Nicholson, can become fashion brands if there is a single unifying creative vision for the brand and control over the design, merchandising and marketing of the products. He never does things in half measures and says, 'If you want to build an empire you need to arrive with your army at the same time'. To him energy is the most important thing in life. He's 50 and had a heart attack 4 years ago. 'I was dead on the counter and nothing was moving,' he says. 'I woke up a day later and I thought I would not be able to work anymore.' He's now determined to make the next 20 years of his career really count. To him now everything is possible. **'We French say that impossible is not French.' Insist to exist.**

[4]Three large US chains of shops: Neiman Marcus is high-end, Bloomingdales is more affordable and Target is all about value.

ACCIDENTS WILL HAPPEN (IT'S ALWAYS HIT AND RUN)

'I have not failed. I've just found 10,000 ways that won't work.'
Thomas Edison

Here's a conundrum: can a business be both efficient and creative? Can it have processes in place that enable it to deliver goods or services at a profit, and still allow enough leeway to take the risks and make the mistakes that being innovative requires? This is something many businesses struggle with. 3M is known as an innovation powerhouse, but its invention of the Post-it note is a long way in the past.[5] 3M CEO George Buckley, in trying to recreate the culture of innovation that existed in the company's heyday, recognises that efficiency programmes might need to take a back seat. **'Invention is by its very nature a disorderly process,'** he says.[6] 'You can't put a Six Sigma process into that area and say, well, I'm getting behind on invention, so I'm going to schedule myself for three good ideas on Wednesday and two on Friday. That's not how creativity works.' He's referring to Six Sigma, a business-management strategy originally developed by Motorola to identify and remove the causes of errors and defects in manufacturing and business processes. Specially trained experts in the disciplines of Six Sigma are called 'Black Belts' – and boy are they tough. Hi-yah!

[5]About 30 years in the past, in fact. Art Fry and Spencer Silver developed it over a number of years during the 1970s and it finally went into full production in 1980.

[6]'At 3M, A Struggle Between Efficiency and Creativity: How CEO George Buckley is managing the yin and yang of discipline and imagination', Brian Hindo, *Business Week*, 11 June 2007.

In the 3M of old, much like the Google of today, employees were actively encouraged to develop their own independent pet projects and apply for funding for them from sources within the company. Risk and failure were accepted as part of the '3M way'. Art Fry, inventor of the Post-it note, questions whether his innovation would have ever seen the light of day in an environment that embraces efficiency over experimentation. His view is that, **'Innovation is a numbers game. You have to go through 5,000 to 6,000 raw ideas to find one successful business.'**[7] Six Sigma, on the other hand, tries to avoid errors – and it's making errors that makes innovation possible. Marva Collins, a US educator who worked tirelessly to help impoverished students in and around Chicago to get a decent education, said, 'If you can't make a mistake, you can't make anything.'

Many readers will (and just as many won't) remember from school the story of how penicillin was discovered. In 1928, while researching the flu virus, Dr Alexander Fleming (after whom phlegm is named[8]) noticed that some mould had contaminated a flu culture in one of his Petri dishes. Instead of throwing it away, as most house-proud folks would do, he kept it to examine it more closely. Fleming had learned the benefits of scientific breakthrough discovered by chance a few years previously when by accident he had shed a tear on a bacteria sample, only to find that the area around the teardrop became free of bacteria. This led him to discover that the tear contained an antibiotic enzyme that could stave off mild bacterial growth. We don't know why he was crying in the first place, but that's beside the point. The mould on the Petri dish of flu culture piqued his curiosity and through further investigation he found that the mould was lethal to the potent *staphylococcus* bacteria in his dish. The

[7]'At 3M, A Struggle Between Efficiency and Creativitiy', Brian Hindo, *Business Week*, 11 June 2007.

[8]That's not true at all. It comes from the Middle-English word 'fleume'.

mould came from the genus penicillin, and the rest is history (as was the bit before). He won the Nobel Prize in 1945 – all because he cried like a baby in his lab one day. 'But for the previous experience, I would have thrown the plate away, as many bacteriologists had done before,' said Fleming.

The microwave was also invented by chance (not Chance the Gardener,[9] just by chance). When Percy Lebaron Spencer was working on magnetrons, a type of device designed to produce the microwave signals for use in radars, and was standing near a working machine with a bar of chocolate in his pocket (we think he was trying to impress the female researchers in the lab) the chocolate melted and – ping! – the microwave oven was born.

CATCHING SPARKS

All of us come across ideas by chance and we can also create opportunities to make those chances more likely. Good old serendipity. You have to be ready to catch those ideas when they pop into your head. Often they'll seem unrelated to whatever projects you're working on, but you'll be surprised how often they connect at a later date. To stop them floating away you might want to carry around a notebook. Yes, just a regular old-fashioned notebook to jot down notes and ideas. (Moleskine, made by Modo&Modo of Italy, make a lovely range of simple, black covered books just asking to be scribbled in.) **Train yourself to write down any thoughts or ideas in your notebook and then regularly look through it to see if they spark inspiration for what you're working on.**

[9]See section on metaphors in Chapter 6.

Using notebooks can be a way to conduct a group brainstorming over a period of weeks rather than the typical hour or two, letting ideas develop, stew and ferment into a tasty brew. To start with, as always, the problem the group is trying to solve needs to be clearly articulated, maybe written up on the first page of the notebook so participants can refer back to it. Then over the next four weeks the members of the group are each asked to come up with one idea a day to solve the creative problem that has been set. Every few days or so they are given some new piece of relevant information or stimulus to help push their thinking along. At the end of the month the group are tasked with writing down the *one* idea they developed that they consider to be the best to solve the problem, together with some suggestions for further exploration. They should also write down ideas they came up with that seem unrelated to the problem as a way to create an *ideas bank* for future projects.

Another way to use notebooks is to have regular *idea jams*. This is the freestyle jazz of idea creation. People, whether or not they're all working together on the same project, can gather together once a month to share the ideas they've captured in their notebooks. Put people's names in a hat (if they've got into the contemporary jazz mood a few of them will be wearing hats anyway) to see who starts. The chosen one picks an idea or interesting thought from his or her notebook and explains it to the group. Sometimes there'll be murmurs of appreciation or a smattering of applause, sometimes not. Others throw in their take on the idea and add in relevant thoughts from their books that might help build on it.

Having an idea jam in which the people involved aren't working on a specific problem, but instead are just capturing and discussing random ideas, might at first glance seem like a waste of time for a busy business, but we beg to differ. For one, having and sharing ideas just feels good, simple as that, and, for two, idea jams train us to capture and discuss random ideas and so are a great way to explore and hone our creative abilities. And, for three, the ideas discussed might actually lead to something relevant to the business context or even lead to an idea for a valuable subsidiary business. So, go with the flow, man, chill. Oh, and four, businesses that have tried it have had good success. IBM held their first World Jam in 2001 as a three-day web-based moderated group brainstorm. 2006's jam was, according to their website, the biggest brainstorming ever, involving 150,000 people from 104 countries and 67 companies around the world who together posted 46,000 ideas (see our chapter *Kill the Idea* on how to whittle down your ideas). And as a result '10 new IBM businesses were launched with seed investment totaling $100 million.'[10] We salute you, big blue.

CULTURES OF CREATIVITY

'You can't just give someone a creativity injection. You have to create an environment for curiosity and a way to encourage people and get the best out of them,' says creativity expert Sir Ken Robinson. But, 'creating a culture of innovation and creativity in companies is more than just setting up a cool room with creative toys and a whiteboard.'[11] Pixar, the

[10]From the IBM Jam events page **www.collaborationjam.com**

[11]Sir Ken Robinson, quoted in 'Reading, Writing, and Creativity: Education guru Sir Ken Robinson talks about the importance of nurturing innovative solutions in the classroom – indeed, in every aspect of modern life', *Business Week* online, 23 February 2006.

Disney-owned animation studio, is a good example of how to do it right. Employees are entitled to spend four hours each week at what's known as Pixar University, where there are classes, events and workshops throughout the day and the attendees are actively encouraged not to do anything job-related. Cool.

W.L. Gore and Associates is a developer and manufacturer of innovative materials and is most famous for its waterproof and breathable GORE-TEX fabric. **The company encourages its employees to play with new ideas to see what they come up with.** For instance, while Gore had previously nothing to do with the music business, it now has a third of the guitar-string market through its non-breakable guitar strings, Elixir. Elixir was developed by a Gore engineer playing with the cables on his mountain bike to see how he could improve them, which got him thinking about guitar strings, and then led him to team up with another Gore engineer who worked on the non-breakable dental floss, Glide. Lots more playing around and three years later Elixir was born (cautionary note: never floss your teeth or play the guitar while mountain biking).

A study by London Business School researchers[12] investigated how companies like Google, 3M, Pixar and Gore use play in the workplace to stimulate creativity and make possible breakthrough ideas that keep them ahead of the competition. The authors concluded that businesses encourage play in three ways: by creating a playful environment; by allowing employees the freedom, time and resources to make play a part of their work; and by giving them the safety to experiment in areas that aren't necessarily a part of the company's core businesses.

[12]'Ideas are Born in Fields of Play: Towards a Theory of Play and Creativity in Organizational Settings', Charalampos Mainemelis and Sarah Ronson, *Research in Organizational Behavior*, Vol. 27, 2006, pp. 81–131.

But introducing a sense of play in the workplace is not without its challenges. Samsung, the Korean electronics giant, so as to maintain its position as Asia's most valuable technology company, has been trying to implement a more creative culture. Apparently it's not always easy in a culture like Samsung's, where hard work traditionally looks like, well, hard work. In their Value Innovation Programme Centre a little south of Seoul, 'The engineers immediately start tidying up and stacking all the magazines in date order, the R&D people only want to talk with Americans, and the designers just stand there and don't say anything,' says Chung Sue-Young,[13] one of the centre coordinators. It seems to be working, though. At the innovation centre they came up with the wine-glass-shaped Bordeaux flatscreen TV, the first Samsung TV to sell over one million units.

Tero Ojanperä, Executive Vice-President at Nokia, told Business Playground: 'You need to break the traditional linear way of thinking. You need to break the existing departments. You need to bring in new people. You need to figure out the new ways of putting different types of people together.' But, again, he knows it isn't always easy: 'For companies it's really a challenge to put together the different types of people, because very often the like-minded people gravitate together. Engineers talk to engineers. Artists will talk to artists. How can we break that mould? How can we force people who think differently together?' The Nokia Ideas Camp is an attempt to help. Tero says, 'Our Ideas Camp is a step in that direction. We invite really different types of people together with an agenda that gets formed on the spot.'

[13]'Samsung Sows for the Future with its Garden of Delights', Anna Fifield, *Financial Times*, 2 January 2008.

Robert Sutton, Professor of Science and Engineering at Stanford University, supports the notion that creative businesses can make people who are used to more traditional ways of working feel uncomfortable. 'After studying creative companies and teams for more than a decade,' he says,[14] 'I've found them to be remarkably inefficient and often terribly annoying places to work, where "managing by getting out of the way" is often the best approach of all.' He continues, **'Managing for creativity, I've discovered, means taking most of what we know about management and standing it on its head.** It means placing bets on ideas without much heed to the projected ROI [return on investment]. It means ignoring what has worked before. It means taking perfectly happy people and goading them into fights among themselves. Good creativity management means hiring the candidate you have a gut feeling against. And as for those people who stick their fingers in their ears and chant, "I'm not listening, I'm not listening," when customers are making suggestions? It means praising and promoting them.'

Christian Audigier's approach to hiring is simple: 'If people can give me something more creative than my ideas I'll take them. I love to drink all this stuff.' He often hires them, not based upon experience, but on their *willingness to try new things*. Professor Sutton is a strong believer in hiring people for innovative businesses that are slow at learning the ways things 'should be done'. Instead of fitting in too easily, they should question and rebel and create waves. He tells the story of the guy who invented the laser printer at Xerox, Gary Starkweather. Over many months he pushed and pushed for the use of lasers rather than white light to 'paint' images for document copying, despite repeated objections by researchers and bosses who were convinced it wasn't the way to go. Eventually, when the department he was working with could stand his dogged persistence no longer, he was transferred to a new research facility. When the

[14]'The Weird Rules of Creativity', Robert Sutton, *Harvard Business Review*, September 2001.

Xerox laser printer he helped develop was finally launched it became one of company's best-selling products. If Mr Starkweather had just 'fitted in' and followed instructions to drop his pursuit of lasers, the Xerox laser printer would never have come about.

A recent IBM/Economist report entitled 'The Enterprise of the Future'[15] says that for businesses to successfully meet the challenges of what in the future will be certain change, there need to be: 'visionary challengers – people who question assumptions and suggest radical, and what some might initially consider, impractical, alternatives.' Danny Socolof, the veteran music industry deal-maker, talked about the 'internal entrepreneurs' who drive change in large corporations by taking risks, sometimes without having been given express permission to do so (see Chapter 3).

Hiring people from different backgrounds and with different perspectives and skills helps keep things fresh. But **it's not just the variety of people that matters; an individual might have multiple social identities that provide new points of view.** Research by Jeffrey Sanchez-Burks, Fiona Lee and Chi-Ying Cheng[16] focuses on people who have 'multiple social identities', for instance, being both Asian and American or both women and engineers. They found that individuals with multiple social identities like these show higher levels of creativity for problems that make use of the knowledge that comes through their different perspectives. An environment in which female engineers aren't forced to suppress their femininity by dressing like men, for instance, should make them more comfortable with their different social identities and so more creative. (Neither should male engineers be pressured into dressing like women, but what they do at the weekend is totally up to them.)

[15]'The Enterprise of the Future: Global CEO Study', conducted by IBM and The Economist Intelligence Unit, 2008.

[16]'Identity Integration and Innovation', Chi-Ying Cheng, Jeffrey Sanchez-Burks and Fiona Lee, Ross School of Business Working Paper series, March 2007.

"I live in Los Angeles and when I'm at home rather than off travelling somewhere, I go to work everyday around 11a.m. to my offices and the studio I share with my great friend, Glen Ballard. My offices are on the fifth floor and have been described[17] as a cross between Willy Wonka's Factory and Andy Warhol's Factory.[18] My factory is an ideas factory called 'Weapons of Mass Entertainment' (WME). There are no real office rules or guidelines, we just have ideas and either make them work quickly or put them aside (we never throw them away, although sometimes I give them away, either wittingly or unwittingly!). There is no regular day and the staff know that at any moment I could arrive with anyone from John Williams (producer of the film *Shrek*, among others), to Marvin Jarrett (the editor of *Nylon* magazine), or Colbie Caillait (a young singer-songwriter) … or perhaps the CEO of a technology company.

In fact, during the day there is an endless stream of creative people in and out of the office, and many different topics are discussed, from animated feature films, to online transparent payment systems, to song choruses. At all times staff will wander in and out and join in on the conversations, or just carry on working with headphones on and eyes glued to computer screens. My company is a creative company and, hey, guess what, I employ creative people. They include Kori Bundi, a young filmmaker and editor; Dave Harris, a scriptwriter and researcher; Ned Douglas, an amazing music programmer, writer and engineer; Tony Quinn, who can literally do anything you ask him (and competed in the world kick-boxing championships); Jamie Bryant, a young visual artist; Nick Corcorran, a writer and filmmaker; Angela Vicari, who spins 12 plates doing things like schedules for *GHOST* musical workshops and film company meetings, setting up events, and even creating the posters; Faithe Dillman, who only needs one hour's sleep yet is a whirling dervish and can text on two phones at once; and Allison Bond, receptionist and project coordinator. We also have an army of legal experts and business advisors and numerous talented individuals we bring in on a project-by-project basis.

As well as inventing and running projects, we also manage some upcoming artists

[17]The *Los Angeles Times* described the offices as 'a media company for the new world'.

[18]Andy Warhol's New York studio was called The Factory. The original one – later ones were also known as The Factory – that he had from 1962–68 was on the fifth floor of 231 East 47th Street, in Manhattan, and attracted a mix of musicians, artists and filmmakers.

such as Nadirah X, a rap artist, singer and actress Cindy Gomez, virtuoso violinist Anne-Marie Calhoun, actress and singer Natalie Mendoza, and A Girl Called Boy. What's amazing about our office is that everyone can join in the discussions, even though it may not be their field of expertise. In fact, often the artists we manage join in on the discussions on other projects we are doing at WME, even work on the projects or do research for us, and have been known to act as chauffeurs, driving me to meetings, or answering the phones! Basically, it's a madhouse. If anyone thought 'the lunatics have taken over the asylum', then this is the place where it rings true. Yet we happen to be working with some of the largest companies in the world, plus we have a real martini bar in the office, so we can't be that crazy.

Upstairs on the sixth floor are the studios and edit suites that I share with Glen Ballard. At first glance this looks a lot more calm and serene. But, don't be fooled, this also is a madhouse, with Glen and me working on at least ten music projects together at the same time, as well as on our own separate projects. Glen is as methodical as I am impetuous, so we make a great team. As well as Glen being a genius songwriter and producer,[19] he is also a perfect collaborative partner who always listens to ideas and digests them before forming an opinion. He also knows how important it is to let 'idea spaghetti' tumble out of my head and not to stop the flow. Glen and I will never run out of things to write songs about or have nothing going on in the studio because we are two 'radiators'. You see there are 'drains' and 'radiators' in this world and if you are in a business that needs creative input (which is *all* businesses), it's best to hire 'radiators' rather than 'drains' and something we call 'FPP' (Fast Positive People).

A good example of how Glen and I work together was on a children's film called *Charlotte's Web*, based on the Pulitzer Prize-winning book. We were asked to write the title song for the film and readily accepted as it's a great book and Dakota Fanning was playing the lead. Plus Burt Berman, a great movie music man, was steering the ship and the last time I worked with Burt, Mick Jagger and I won a Golden Globe for best song in a movie.[20] Glen and I met with Burt and the director and discussed the book and how it was going to be interpreted for the big screen. When we left the meeting we both knew that writing a song about a pig

[19]Glen produced Alanis Morissette's amazing 1995 album *Jagged Little Pill*, which has sold more than 30 million copies worldwide.

[20]*Old Habits Die Hard* was a song for the 2004 film *Alfie*, which won the 2005 Golden Globe for Best Original Song.

and a spider was not going to be easy, but we were pretty confident we would come up with something. The day Glen and I were meant to go see a first rough cut, Glen was sick with the flu bug so I went on our behalf and, halfway through the screening, I sent a text message to Glen saying the song should be called *Ordinary Miracle*. Before I got back to the studio Glen sent me an audio file with the first verse melody and singing lyrics, and it was sounding perfect. I sent a message back saying, 'Great, don't change a thing' – you see he had already cracked the code and, as his teammate, I was cheering him on and excited to join in.

Once we had made a template or blueprint of the whole song, with me singing the demo, and after it had been 'analysed' by the film studio (which is a bit like being on trial for armed robbery), we got the song green-lit. We both really wanted Sarah McLachlan to sing it so we sent her a rough version, and she liked it, so we hopped on a plane to Vancouver with Sam Schwartz, our film agent, Burt Berman and the legendary Randy Spendlove to record Sarah in her beautiful home studio in the woods. I wanted a video with Dakota Fanning miming the words sitting at the piano with Sarah's voice coming out of her mouth. I thought that would be odd and get people's attention,

especially children around the world. But they made a straightforward video of Sarah at the piano intercut with the movie.

Now when you write a song and it's finished and exists, it becomes a business in itself – a kind of 'song brand' – and in fact a huge business would be to manage these 'song brands' properly. For instance, *Sweet Dreams* as a song is known in every country around the world. It's much better known than Annie or myself. If I walked up to most strangers in any country and sang, 'Sweet Dreams are Made of This', they would say, 'I know that song,' but would not necessarily know Eurythmics or Annie Lennox or Dave Stewart. This song *Ordinary Miracle* became a phenomenon on the web and if you type it in YouTube you will see thousands of people making their own video to it, of their child being born, or of beautiful landscapes, or of a school choir singing it.[21] Songs as 'intellectual property' (IP) are not unlike software or other trademarked inventions that get licensed for a fee or a royalty, and the creative process that goes into writing a song is pretty similar to the creative process that goes into solving many problems. It's like a jigsaw puzzle or a code that needs to be cracked, the only difference being that songwriting usually includes personal emotional storytelling as part of the puzzle.

[21]It also became the theme song on a commercial for the CVS pharmacy chain in US.

MONEY, THAT'S WHAT I WANT ...?

How important are money and other extrinsic rewards, such as job title and recognition, in motivating individuals to want to produce creative work? Glad you asked. **Evidence from various studies suggests that when people think they are going to be rewarded for creativity, they are in fact more creative.** In the words of Bobbi Flekman, the hostess with the mostess in Rob Reiner's film *This is Spinal Tap*, 'money walks and bullshit talks'. The data backs this up. A review of existing studies by one researcher showed that, 'The expectation that creativity will be rewarded causes individuals to define the task as requiring creativity, to become immersed in it, and to search for novel ways of carrying it out.'[22] And in contrast, if people think a reward depends on them performing without using creativity, that's what they'll do – be less creative.

Of course, as you might expect, it's not quite that simple. While extrinsic rewards, such as cold hard cash, play a very important role, the *intrinsic* rewards – things like intellectual curiosity or seeing a creative task as a personal challenge – are also big drivers of creativity. One research paper looked at the relationship between the number of patents filed – an indication of creative output – and the individual motivations of the workers who created the innovations that were patented. Data[23] collected from more than 11,000 US research and development (R&D) employees in manufacturing and service companies showed that the R&D folk involved in the early-stage types of research (more R than D) were more productive if

---

[22]'Rewards, Intrinsic Motivation, and Creativity: A Case Study of Conceptual and Methodological Isolation', R. Eisenberger and L. Shanock, *Creativity Research Journal*, 2003.

[23]People were surveyed by the National Science Foundation.

motivated by the intellectual challenge of the task, and a degree of independence was more important for them than it was for workers involved in later stages (more D than R).

How people perceive their work environments unsurprisingly has an effect on their creativity. According to an extensive study using workers' diary entries as data,[24] 'People were over 50 per cent more likely to have creative ideas on the days they reported the most positive moods than they were on other days,' and, 'the more positive a person's mood on a given day, the more creative thinking he or she did the next day – and, to some extent, the day after that.' If they see work in a positive light – you know, good bosses, collaborative spirit, focused on a creative vision, being rewarded for creativity – they are more likely to be creative than when things were screwed up – infighting, an aversion to new ideas and taking risks – in which cases their creative juices sort of dry up. So, yes Bobbi, while money does indeed talk, if people aren't into what they're doing, the bullshit walks.

[24]'Inner Work Life: Understanding the Subtext of Business Performance', Teresa M. Amabile and Steven J. Kramer, *Harvard Business Review*, May 2007, looked at over 12,000 diary entries from 238 professionals in different work teams.

THE BUSINESS PLAYGROUND CREATIVITY QUOTIENT (BPCQ) TEST

As there is IQ, or Intelligence Quotient, as a measure of how intelligent (whatever that means) people are, it stands to reason there should be CQ, or Creativity Quotient, as a measure of how creative they are. Of course, creativity already has an obvious measure: the output that a person creates. Lots of amazing piano concertos suggests creativity. Piles of great canvases, creative too. Shelves of wonderful novels – yup, creative. But just looking at creative output isn't enough, for a couple of reasons. First, who's to say whether any of the things created are actually any good? (As we said way earlier in the book, they have to be both unique and useful rather than just notes on a staff, blobs on a canvas, or words on a page.) And, second, while all ideas should have some manifestation (a thing that comes as a result of it) creative output is rarely so clear-cut or simple as an object that expresses an idea or set of ideas. **In business, the things that our creative talents contribute to might be a system, or a business model, or a way of thinking about something, and it almost always involves collaboration between many, many people.**

There are tests that specifically try to measure creativity – the Torrance Tests of Creative Thinking developed by psychologist Paul Torrance being one notable example – but we felt the world could do with one more. The Business Playground Creative Quotient (we couldn't get a really snappy acronym from those letters so for now we're calling it BPCQ) is designed not to tell people how creative they are being, but to inform them how creative they can be if they open their minds to the possibilities.

Why not take our simple test to see what your BPCQ score is.

1 Being distracted by something unrelated to a problem can help you solve the problem. So imagine you are getting on a bus to take a short journey, one that will let your body and mind wander. Do you:

   a. Head towards the bench seat at the back?

   b. Sit near the driver so you can see the people getting on and off?

   c. Get your biscuits out of your bag before sitting down?

   d. Change your mind and get on to a different bus going on another route?

   e. Talk to the woman in the green hat?

   (Answer: it doesn't matter, so long as you leave your problem behind for a few hours.)

2 Half the battle is deciding what is the question you're trying to answer through creativity. If you are a baker trying to make more money, which questions help your thinking?

   a. How can I create bread that is even better than sliced bread?

   b. How can I increase sales of my bread?

   c. How can I increase the profit margins for my bread?

   d. What else can I sell that will make me some bread?

   e. Are there any job openings as a candlestick maker in the area?

   (Answer: a, b, c and d are all good questions and worth exploring, but as each is a very different take on the bigger problem of making more money and demands different creative solutions, pick one at a time. Being a candlestick maker is a possibility, but might require some retraining.)

3 Corporate environments are rarely very conducive ones for identifying and executing big ideas. You find yourself in the lift with the CEO and want to tell her your idea that you've been trying to get through the bureaucracy below her for months. Would you:

   a. Jam your finger on the emergency stop button and make your pitch at your leisure?

   b. Blurt it out as quickly as you can, not knowing how long it will be before she gets out, or others get in?

   c. Make a friendly comment about the stock price and then say nothing else?

   d. Ask her for 10 minutes of her time at another date?

   e. Do none of these things then kick yourself metaphorically and in reality when you leave the lift?

   (Answer: We don't know, it's a tough one. Option d sounds like the most sensible, options a and b only happen in cheesy movies and options c and e are what most people do, and who can blame them given the way most corporations focus on efficiency at the expense of creativity?)

4 Quantity of novel ideas generated is more important than quality, at least in the early stages of the creative process. We call this idea spaghetti. If the problem is *finding creative uses for a household brick*, how many ideas can you come up with for a brick in two minutes, starting now?

   a. 21–40.

   b. 9–19.

   c. 40+.

   d. Less than 2.

   e. 21 exactly.

(Answer: either a or c would be good, b is so-so and e would just be weird!)

5 Drawing diagrams and pictures can help us think through problems creatively by tapping into a different part of the brain, one that relies less on our abilities to process language. Is it best to:

   a. Take a furry pencil case with you wherever you go, one that is full of brightly coloured pens and pencils?

   b. Hire a professional sketch artist to sit in during brainstorming sessions to capture comments and ideas?

   c. Take time to sit and think with a piece of paper to sketch your thoughts on?

   d. Draw caricatures of your work colleagues while they're talking?

   e. Add doodles to important documents?

(Answer: Option c for sure. Option a works if it's a great pencil case and b sometimes works if the sketch artists are good and you know how to use what they've done. Options d and e are fine if you want to get fired quickly. Creating isn't always about just sitting staring at a computer screen, and in fact sitting at a computer screen can distract us from genuine thinking, so get a pad and start sketching out what's on your mind.)

6 Humour and creativity are closely linked, as jokes and ideas are both ways of looking at the world in unexpected ways. Pick two or more of the following to create a joke that connects them:

   a. A nun.

   b. A penguin.

   c. A fish.

   d. A prostitute.

   e. A pair of knickers.

(Answer: If you laughed merely at the thought of combining some of these ideas then you see what we mean, it's funny!)

7 Doing certain activities before being creative can boost our performance. Which ones of these have been shown to work?

   a. Aerobic exercise.

   b. Playing certain videogames.

   c. Listening to music.

   d. Filing your taxes and your nails.

   e. Having sex.

(Answer: Options a, b and c, either by increasing blood flow to our brains or improving our mood, or in some cases both. Having sex must work too, but we couldn't find any scientific studies that tested it.)

8 Coming up with ideas in groups in the form of brainstorms is sometimes counterproductive, with the number and quality of ideas produced being less than when people work individually. Which of these techniques helps make brainstorming sessions more productive?

a. Setting the goals very high.

b. Using doughnuts as a way to increase the blood-sugar levels.

c. Ridiculing any suggestions other than one's own, either with a verbal put-down or just a snort of contempt.

d. Making the mix of people less homogenous by including people from varying backgrounds, skills and identities.

e. All being naked with the lights off.

(Answer: Definitely a and d, but we suspect option e might work too.)

9 Creating the right environment for the creative juices involves more than how creative the space you're working in looks. Which one of these things is the odd one out because it doesn't help bring out our creative abilities?

a. Being paid cold hard cash as an incentive.

b. The boss giving clear goals for what is expected from a project.

c. Feeling good about the work you're doing.

d. A positive collaborative environment.

e. Being allowed to wear big clown shoes to the office.

(Answer: you guessed it, b. Sorry, we meant e.)

10 What's the best idea you've ever heard, either old or new, yours or someone else's? Write it down and answer the following questions about it:

a. What is the fundamental human need it solves?

b. What two existing elements did it connect in a new way?

c. What do you think the barriers were/are to making it happen?

d. What combination of factors made/ might make it possible?

e. Knowing what you know, how would you have done/do it differently?

(Great! If it's a new idea that nobody's done yet, send it our way.)

ROLL THE DICE TO PICK A PREVIOUS CHAPTER

Bringing ideas to life and taking them from a vision to action without getting too hung up on hallucination requires having an incredible amount of perseverance and self-belief. It also means being surrounded by great people. **A creative culture is one in which people aren't just rewarded for successes, but are allowed and actively encouraged to experiment and make mistakes.** We can create environments to make those chance ideas more likely by doing simple things like keeping notebooks for capturing ideas and conducting idea jam sessions that demonstrate a system-wide commitment to brave ideas; by embracing playfulness and risk-taking; and by hiring people in the organisation who go against the grain and even don't seem to fit. People are motivated to be creative in organisations by extrinsic rewards like money, recognition and even just the expectation of needing to be creative, and by intrinsic rewards such as the personal challenge or by intellectual curiosity, and the best business playground depends on creating the right mix of these things in a collaborative environment with a shared clear vision.

Instructions

1. Pick the one idea you want to launch.
2. You have 30 minutes to write a launch plan for it.
3. Give your idea a name and a look.
4. Write it up as a news story explaining the idea, what it does and who it's for.
5. Describe who else you can bring in to collaborate with to make it happen.

What's my mission?

What am I called?

Who is on the crew?

BOARD GAME: BLAST OFF!

How it works: Launching your idea is as important as coming up with it in the first place! So without much further ado, let's start the countdown and get it into orbit. Commencing countdown, engines on.

Ten … nine … eight …

In this game players have to quickly choose *just one* from a bunch of ideas, make sure all the pieces are in place and then launch it into the market.

Seven … six … five …

You won't know if it's exactly the right idea, but the time is ripe for a bit of exploration into the unknown.

Four … three … two … one.

Blast off!

How to play: When in 1948 Albert became the first monkey in space he was charting unknown territory. Unfortunately, he died of suffocation during the flight. But, that aside, he was a pioneer! And a shade under 11 years and a few dozen monkeys later Able and Miss Baker, a rhesus monkey and a squirrel monkey, became the first living creatures to go into space and successfully return to Earth. In the next few years, a collection of chimps, mice, guinea pigs, frogs, rats, cats, a few insects, a tortoise and some dogs followed them up. In fact, by the time Yuri Gagarin, a Russian and a human, went into space in 1961 pretty much the whole animal world had taken a

look. So here's a nod of acknowledgement to little Albert and his bravery in going for it. We raise a banana to you.

Now it's your turn to go into the unknown, this time without suffocating, we hope. The game involves quickly choosing one of your ideas and doing some of the things you'd need to do if you were going to launch it for real, by giving your idea a clear mission, a story and a crew who can help make it happen.

From ideas they've already generated, players choose quickly just one, based on gut instinct or even just randomly (the *Kill the Idea* game is a good way to hone in on one). The decision has to be made quickly, the countdown has begun. Now we're going to bring the idea to life by deciding what to call it, how to pitch it and who to involve to make it work. And all within 30 minutes.

Who am I? To take your idea from words on a scrap of paper we need to give it an identity. A name, however gimmicky, and a sketch or diagram of what it might look like, however scrappy, will make your idea into something that is tangible, one that *you can imagine actually happening*. Come up with a name that communicates the main characteristics of the idea (e.g. Super Glue) or conveys a sense of its purpose (e.g. Nike was the Greek goddess of strength, speed and victory). Think about who it's aimed at, what it will make them feel and how it's better or different from the competition. The sketch can be as simple as a crude line drawing that suggests your idea's form (whether a product, a service or experience).

What's the mission? All ideas have to have a practical application with real goals, a clear plan and criteria for success. Write up the idea as a short news story with a punchy headline and the key details about what the idea is about, what the point of it is and who it's aimed at.

Who is on the crew? It's almost impossible to do it alone: we need to partner with others who buy into our mission and are willing to help us accomplish it. Make a list of the people (or monkeys) in your organisation and from the outside who you can collaborate with to launch your idea.

How to win: Create a full launch plan within 30 minutes.

Now let's go and launch an idea for real!

'Twenty years from now you will be more disappointed by the things that you didn't do than by the ones you did do. So throw off the bowlines. Sail away from the safe harbor. Catch the trade winds in your sails. Explore. Dream. Discover.'
Mark Twain

CONCLUSION

Kids have got it right. They explore and play, have fun and come up with ideas. In the children's book *Not A Box*, by Antoinette Portis, a rabbit is asked why he is sitting on, or standing on, or spraying or wearing a cardboard box, and drawings show what the questioner sees … a rabbit and a box. 'It's not a box,' he insists each time. To him it's a racing car, a mountain, a burning building or a robot, and simple lines added to the illustrations reveal how in his mind the box has been transformed.

Business Playground is about how us grown-ups can rediscover the magic of creativity that we all lived and breathed every day as children, and apply it to business. Creativity is not just a nice to have; in a constantly changing world in which a business is only as good as its latest innovation, it has become an absolute necessity. But, it can be scary. Developing and executing new ideas requires taking leaps into the unknown and is often hit and miss, and creativity doesn't always easily fit into a corporate environment where efficiency is king and mistakes must be avoided at all costs.

It may be tempting to outsource it, or to keep it quarantined off in a separate part of the building where only people with special clearance can go, but the very nature of creativity means that it's unpredictable and we cannot know when it might have an impact. So we need to make it a part of everyday business. Luckily, help is at hand. **Business Playground is full of examples of how highly creative people think and includes techniques and games that can help get our creative muscles trained and ready for action.** Throughout the previous chapters …

We learned that when we allow ourselves to move outside the expected, creative brilliance is possible and, although education and work stifle our natural creative talents, they remain and can be brought out to play once more.

We realised that size really does matter and that how many ideas we can come up with – *idea spaghetti* – makes it more likely that some of them will be good ones, and that we need to think divergently to stimulate the creation of lots of ideas.

We looked at how not accepting the status quo is a great starting point for innovation, how there are always things to improve upon – whether it's the design of a product or the way a whole industry works – and about the value of being constantly curious.

We wondered how asking the right questions might give us a better chance of coming up with the right solutions. We need to question the assumptions we're making about a business problem and get rid of the ones that don't hold true, and we need to explore different ways of framing a problem and break it down into manageable chunks.

We uncovered a lot of scientific evidence about the conditions in which the creative thought process works most effectively, and how temporarily taking our minds off problems we're trying to solve creatively can actually help. Music, exercise and playing games put us in a positive mood and this has a positive effect on our creative abilities.

We saw that visualising can help free up creative thinking that might otherwise have been restricted if we had relied solely on words, and that there are wonderful techniques, including drawing sketches, taking photographs and using similes and metaphors to spark ideas.

We embraced the idea of playing with others in a collaborative way and the importance of having leaders that have clear visions which they communicate well and who will help the team members understand their individual roles in making it happen.

We made ourselves think BIG in order to break free of expected ideas and saw how evocative language is a powerful way of bringing a problem to life and focusing creative energy on it.

We tried on some other people's shoes to see what they felt like and how looking at a problem from fresh perspectives can prevent ourselves being limited by what we already know.

We conducted a little orchestrated chaos and randomness to connect things together and create something new and unexpected, and saw how humour can change the direction of our thinking when it's getting a little stale.

We murdered any ideas that weren't worth spending time and effort on to focus on those that were, by looking at practical considerations and also by using our gut instincts to pick winners.

And, lastly, we explored what it takes to put our ideas into orbit, how it takes perseverance and self-belief and being surrounded by great people working in a creative culture to encourage experimentation and risk.

So, we hope you've enjoyed the journey and have had a chance to play some of the games dotted throughout the book, and we hope you have been inspired to put some of your creative skills to work in your business. Please visit us at **www.businessplayground.com**

We're going to finish with a song courtesy of Bob Dylan.

May God bless and keep you always,
May your wishes all come true,
May you always do for others
And let others do for you.
May you build a ladder to the stars
And climb on every rung,
May you stay forever young,
Forever young, forever young,
May you stay forever young.

May you grow up to be righteous,
May you grow up to be true,
May you always know the truth
And see the lights surrounding you.
May you always be courageous,
Stand upright and be strong,
May you stay forever young,
Forever young, forever young,
May you stay forever young.

May your hands always be busy,
May your feet always be swift,
May you have a strong foundation
When the winds of changes shift.
May your heart always be joyful,
May your song always be sung,
May you stay forever young,
Forever young, forever young,
May you stay forever young.

Dave & Mark, May 2010

Answers to the Scavenger Game

The treasure is buried at grid reference I, 9 and here's why:

One: There are 6 Fs, so move 2 spaces anticlockwise to number 9.

Two: The green traffic light is at the bottom, so move 4 spaces anticlockwise to number 5.

Three: There are 3 curves on a paperclip, so move 1 space clockwise to number 6.

Four: It's in her right hand, so move 5 spaces clockwise to number 1.

Five: They rotate clockwise, so move 8 spaces clockwise to number 9.

Six: There are 6 sides, so move 3 spaces clockwise to number 2.

Seven: They are on the left hand pages, so move 7 spaces clockwise to number 9.

Eight: It is red, so move 3 spaces anticlockwise to number 6.

Nine: There are none on the 1, so move 2 spaces clockwise to number 8.

Ten: It's the left, so move 1 space clockwise to number 9.

Eleven: It's the ace of spades, so move 2 spaces anticlockwise to number 5.

Twelve: There are 5 differences, so move 9 spaces anticlockwise to number 9.

Space number 8 leads to the 'X' located at grid reference I, 9.

List of common suggestions for what to do with a paperclip

- Use it as a key-ring.
- Push the reset button on electronic gadgets.
- An emergency toothpick.
- Making snakes.
- Linking them together to make a necklace or bracelet.
- Voodoo paperclip dolls.
- Hang cards from a chain of them.
- Use to clean fingernails and toenails.
- To clean ears with.
- For picking locks.
- Magnetise them together to make sculptures.
- Clean up the grout between bathroom tiles.
- Pop balloons.
- For making cheese and pineapple sticks.
- As tiny chopsticks.
- For a replacement fuse.
- As a hair clip.
- Do-it-yourself ear piercing.
- Hang decorations or Christmas ornaments from them.
- As curtain hooks.
- Make fake specs for stuffed animals.
- As a replacement zipper puller.
- A bookmark.
- An emergency wedding ring.
- For unblocking plug holes.

INDEX